Chris Hani

OHIO SHORT HISTORIES OF AFRICA

This series of Ohio Short Histories of Africa is meant for those who are looking for a brief but lively introduction to a wide range of topics in African history, politics, and biography, written by some of the leading experts in their fields.

Chris Hani

Hugh Macmillan

OHIO UNIVERSITY PRESS

ATHENS

Ohio University Press, Athens, Ohio 45701
www.ohioswallow.com

First published by Jacana Media (Pty) Ltd in 2014
10 Orange Street
Sunnyside
Auckland Park 2092
South Africa
+2711 628 3200
www.jacana.co.za

First published in North America in 2021 by Ohio University Press
Printed in the United States of America
Ohio University Press books are printed on acid-free paper ⊗ ™

Paperback ISBN: 978-0-8214-2454-4
e-ISBN: 978-0-8214-4740-6

Cover art by Joey Hi-Fi

See a complete list of Ohio University titles at ohioswallow.com

... I recall that it is a **communist** as such, a **communist** as **communist**, whom a Polish emigrant and his accomplices, all the assassins of Chris Hani, put to death a few days ago, April 10th [1993]. The assassins themselves said that they were out to get a communist. They were trying to interrupt negotiations and sabotage an ongoing democratization. This popular hero of the resistance against Apartheid became dangerous and suddenly intolerable, it seems, at the moment in which, having decided to devote himself once again to a minority Communist Party riddled with contradictions, he gave up important responsibilities in the ANC and perhaps any official or even governmental role he might one day have held in a country freed of Apartheid.

– JACQUES DERRIDA, SPECTERS OF MARX

'Socialism is the future.'
– CHRIS HANI

'Chris Hani was the future of this country.
They murdered the future.'
– CARLOS MAS ABALA, CUBAN ENVOY

Contents

Introduction

The assassination of Chris Hani outside his home in Dawn Park, a suburb of Boksburg, near Johannesburg, on 10 April 1993 by a right-wing extremist was a decisive moment in the transition to democracy in South Africa. Nelson Mandela's appeal for calm on prime-time television that evening demonstrated that he alone, and not the incumbent president, F.W. de Klerk, had the authority and stature to lead South Africa at a moment of real crisis. Referring to Hani's assassin and the woman who reported the number of his car, resulting in his arrest, he said: 'A white man, full of prejudice and hate, came to our country and committed a deed so foul that our whole nation now teeters on the brink of disaster. A white woman, of Afrikaner origin, risked her life so that we may know, and bring to justice, this assassin.'

Speaking at his funeral on 19 April, Joe Slovo said: 'Chris Hani was killed by those who would like to see an explosion of carnage and race war, a massive spilling of blood, and the end of negotiations. The assassins want to drag us back to a military battlefield. Let us draw them back to a battlefield of our choosing – the battlefield of the ballot. They may have the guns. But we have the majority. Chris Hani had a dream of democracy. They killed the man, but they can never kill the dream. And the dream of Chris Hani is about to become a reality.'

On the same occasion, Nelson Mandela said: 'To lose Chris at this time, when a man of his capabilities is so much needed in this country, will not be forgotten. He was a fighter for peace, freedom and justice. Above all, he was a lover of the poor, the workers and the rural masses. He was a true son of the soil.'

Hani's death added urgency to the search for solutions. Cyril Ramaphosa recalled that after Hani's death 'we went in for the kill'. At a meeting with De Klerk later in April, Mandela demanded a date for democratic elections. Within a few months a transitional constitution was agreed and democratic elections were held on 27 April 1994, a date which marked the formal end of apartheid.

It is the purpose of this book to explain how it was that a man from a remote corner of the Transkei, who had never held high office, was held in such high esteem by so many people. I suggest that it was his conspicuous displays of both physical and moral courage, taken together with compassion and humanity, which combined to make him a great leader.

1

Roots in the Eastern Cape

Chris Hani was born on 28 June 1942 at what was, from the point of view of the enemies of Nazism-Fascism, the low point of the Second World War. On the day of his birth, Hitler's army of occupation in the Soviet Union launched its advance towards Stalingrad, which was to be the site of its later defeat in the decisive battle of the war. In the previous week 10,000 South African soldiers of the Second Division, British Eighth Army, including more than 1,000 black troops of the Native Military Corps, had surrendered to German forces under General Erwin Rommel at Tobruk. The fall of Singapore to Japan in February 1942 and the subsequent occupation of much of South East Asia were major setbacks. The Japanese invasion of Burma threatened India and its attack on the British naval base at Colombo in Ceylon (now Sri Lanka) in April threatened the Indian Ocean. Considerations of 'Native' loyalty in the event of a threat to South Africa prompted the suspension of the hated pass laws in the country's major cities in May 1942 – they were to remain in abeyance until 1946.

Martin Thembisile (which means 'promised' in isiXhosa) Hani, better known as Chris, was born at Lower Sabalele in the district of St Mark's (now Cofimvaba), in the Transkei (now part of the Eastern Cape Province). With an area as large as Basutoland and Swaziland combined, and a much bigger population, the Transkeian Territories formed the largest block of land in African occupation in South Africa. A classic labour reserve, the area exported workers and imported food to supplement the crops that were grown by the permanently resident population of older men, women and children. They were dependent on remittances from workers on the mines and in the factories of the Transvaal, on the sugar plantations of Natal, and in the city of Cape Town, but there was also some cash income from the sale of wool from the large flocks of sheep that grazed the rolling hills. Although poverty was endemic it was not uniform as some families, including Chris Hani's, had cattle, which provided milk and draught power for ploughing, and sheep were unevenly distributed. St Mark's was a drought-prone district where the crops sometimes failed completely, as they did in 1951–52, when Chris Hani was nine. In times of drought the women of Sabalele had to walk long distances to collect water and they often had to go even further to collect firewood. The nearest large store was at St Mark's, which was about 15 kilometres away. The nearest town of any size was Queenstown, about 60 kilometres away in 'white' South Africa, and the nearest railway was the siding at Imvani on the line between Queenstown and East London.

From the early 20th century onwards, the area was administered by the South African Native Affairs Department through chiefs and headmen, and a system of representative councils, which had at their apex the Transkeian General Council, or Bunga. The long-serving headman in the Sabalele area, Gqoboza Ndarala, died in the week of Chris Hani's birth. The acknowledged paramount chief, or king, in Chris Hani's youth was the young Sabata Dalindyebo and the senior chief in St Mark's district was Kaiser Matanzima, who was 26 at the time of Hani's birth. There was an extensive system of mission schools in the Transkei that provided a good basic education for many of the men who became South Africa's prominent black leaders in the second half of the 20th century, including Nelson Mandela, Oliver Tambo, Walter Sisulu, Govan Mbeki, and his son Thabo, the future president, who was born the week before Hani and about 100 kilometres to the east. Lower Sabalele lies halfway between two mission stations, the old-established Anglican mission at St Mark's and the newer Catholic mission at Zigudu. The disproportionate number of black leaders who emerged from the Transkei was a reflection of the quality of the school system, but may also have been the result of the self-confidence young men acquired growing up in an overwhelmingly African area.

Chris Hani was the third surviving child of Gilbert

'Hendesi' Hani and his wife, Mary 'Nomaysie' Hani. He described his father, who was born in 1910, as 'semi-literate', but he was well educated by the standards of his time. He had passed standard six, the last of eight years of primary school, a considerable achievement at a time when very few pupils proceeded to secondary school, and he was able to speak and write English fluently. He worked at first as a labour migrant on the mines, then in the construction industry, and, latterly, as a self-employed trader in Cape Town. When Chris Hani was six years old, in 1948, his father applied for a licence to set up a 'Native' eating house on common land close to his home on the boundary between Upper and Lower Sabalele. He did not pursue the application, but the fact that he made it at all is an indication that he was a man of ambition and enterprise, with some savings, and that he may have sought at that time to abandon labour migration and to make a living at home. But he was away from home for most of his children's formative years, as were the fathers of most of their contemporaries.

In the same year, 1948, the National Party came to power and began to introduce apartheid, a more radical, ruthless and rigid version of the segregation that South Africa's wartime prime minister, General Smuts, had described in 1942 as having 'fallen on evil days'. The introduction of apartheid was soon to have an impact on the Transkei in several ways. The Bantu Authorities Act (1951) was intended to strengthen the power of the chiefs and to lay the foundations for a new system of local government in African areas. In the context of the Transkei the government sought to replace the council system and the Bunga. The strengthening of the administration was intended to make possible the imposition of intensely unpopular 'betterment' measures: to counter soil erosion by compulsory de-stocking, the culling of cattle and sheep, and the reallocation of land and residential sites. These measures were also intended to make room for the removal of African people from nominally 'white' towns and farms and their 'dumping' in the already overcrowded reserves – a process that intensified in the late 1950s, contributing to rural revolts in various parts of South Africa, including Pondoland within the Transkei.

Another disturbing intervention was the Bantu Education Act (1953). This involved the take-over by the state from the Christian missions of the African school system, beginning with primary education in 1955 and culminating with Fort Hare University College in 1959, then the only university college for Africans in the country. There were also changes in the curriculum that were intended to make education for Africans less academic and to reduce the influence on them of the English language, and the culture associated with it, which were seen by Afrikaner nationalists as sources of dangerous liberal and radical ideas. This was part of a systematic campaign to destroy the mission-based, and syncretist, intellectual traditions of the Eastern

Cape, which, as Xolela Mangcu has shown in his recent biography of Steve Biko, had roots going back over three or four generations into the early 19th century.

Chris Hani was an exceptionally bright child who, beginning school in 1950, managed to complete his primary education before the Bantu Education Department take-over and his secondary education before the introduction of retrograde curricular changes. After three or four years at a Catholic primary school at Upper Sabalele, which used the buildings of the local church, he transferred to the Catholic mission at Zigudu, where he remained for a further three or four years. He did his junior certificate exams at Cala (later Matanzima) Secondary School and then transferred to Lovedale, a Church of Scotland school with a strong academic reputation, near the small town of Alice in the Ciskei, where he spent two years studying for the matriculation exams. He had earlier managed to complete standards two and three at Sabalele in one year, and standards five and six at Zigudu in one year. He then achieved a first-class pass in the Senior Certificate exams at the age of 16 – a remarkable feat. He said that he had an advantage over his contemporaries because of the home teaching he received from an aunt who was herself a teacher – she had done four years' education beyond standard six. Members of the Hani family were known locally as *amagqoboka* – the educated ones.

Hani's parents were both baptised, and he was himself christened in the local Catholic Church when ten days old, but he says that they were not practising Christians, and he seems to have discovered religion for himself. He was impressed and strongly influenced by the Catholic priests and sisters at Zigudu and was an altar boy at nine. From the age of 12, and for several years afterwards, he wanted to enter a seminary and train for the priesthood. He was prevented from doing so by his father, who felt that people should look for their reward on earth and not in heaven, a view that he eventually came to share. His mother was also opposed to his becoming a priest, but for a different reason – she wanted grandchildren.

In an interview that he gave shortly before his death to Charles Villa-Vicencio, the editor of a book on religion and politics, he made it clear that he saw a clear thread of continuity, and no contradiction, between his early religious beliefs and his later political convictions. He found the things that originally attracted him to the Church – 'the suffering of the people and the example of the priests in Cofimvaba' – replicated in the African National Congress (ANC) and the South African Communist Party (SACP). As he said: 'My political involvement came as a natural outcome of my religious convictions.'

Chris Hani grew up in a time of political ferment. The ANC launched its Defiance Campaign against unjust apartheid laws in 1952 when he was ten and adopted the Freedom Charter at the Congress of the People in 1955 when he was 13. His father may have been a member of the Communist Party of South Africa (CPSA), and his uncle, Milton Hani, certainly was. He ran a small shop in Khayamandi Township, Stellenbosch, and was also prominent within the ANC in the Western Cape. The brothers both recognised the leadership of Moses Kotane, a leading member of the ANC and the general secretary of the CPSA. It is not, however, clear whether either of them became members of the underground SACP, which was set up in 1953 after the CPSA had been banned in 1950.

Gilbert Hani was on first-name terms with Ray Alexander (Simons), founder of the Food and Canning Workers' Union, and was a close friend of Elizabeth Mafikeng (sometimes spelled Mafekeng), who was also a leader of that union and of the ANC Women's League. He became chairman of the Native Vigilance Association in the Cape Town township of Langa and was a middle-ranking official in the ANC. He was also an organiser among migrant labourers in Cape Town of opposition to the imposition of Bantu Authorities in the Transkei and of an Urban Bantu Council in Langa. He became a prominent opponent of Chief Kaiser Matanzima, who used his support for Bantu Authorities to secure promotion to the status of paramount chief of a new, and essentially bogus, paramountcy – 'Emigrant Tembuland' – which included St Mark's and Sabalele. He was able to prevent Chief Matanzima from addressing a meeting in Langa – the chief had to be given a police escort out of the township, a humiliation for which he never forgave his adversary. In 1962 Gilbert Hani was banished from Cape Town to Sabalele, where he would have been under the watchful eye of Matanzima. He chose to avoid banishment by going into exile at Mafeteng in what was then the British protectorate of Basutoland – it became the independent kingdom of Lesotho four years later. He lived there with Elizabeth Mafikeng, who had gone into exile a little earlier.

Chris Hani became politically aware through the influence of his father and uncle, but also through his teachers and contemporaries at Lovedale. The introduction of Bantu Education was a matter of great concern to the school's staff and also to the students, who were politically organised in a clandestine manner in the face of an authoritarian administration. Hani was at first drawn to the Sons of Young Africa (SOYA), the youth wing of the Non-European Unity Movement, as was his near contemporary, Thabo Mbeki. This group had a strong influence in the Eastern Cape, especially the Transkei, through the Cape African Teachers' Association, which was affiliated with it. They both soon shifted their allegiance to the ANC Youth League, concluding that the Unity Movement was excessively intellectual and elitist. Hani believed that the movement was much more interested in the theory than the practice of revolution. He recalled: 'The struggle was waged in the mind; in the head.' While he was at Lovedale Hani was exposed for the first time to radical and Marxist ideas through reading copies of the Unity Movement's publication, *Torch*, and journals such as *New Age* and *Fighting Talk*, which were edited by Lionel Forman and Ruth First, who were both associated with the SACP. According to one account he was recruited to the ANC by Sipho Makana, later a member of the ANC's National Executive Committee (NEC).

After matriculating at the end of 1958, Hani moved across the Tyhume River in Alice to enter Fort Hare University College, which was then associated with Rhodes University in Grahamstown. In 1959, the year that Hani entered Fort Hare, the college was taken over by the Bantu Education Department and it began the process of transformation from an institution that had drawn students from all over Southern, Eastern and Central Africa into a 'tribal college' for Xhosa-speaking students. Although there was resistance to these changes, including a strike in 1959, Hani managed to survive three years at the college and graduated in 1961 with a pass degree in English and Latin. He also did some law courses. He was able to pay the fees at Fort Hare and to maintain himself with the help of a scholarship from the Bunga, a loan from the Bantu Education Department, and cash contributions from his father, who was then relatively well off. Gilbert Hani had earlier on been able to buy his wife a sewing-machine with which she supplemented her income.

In interviews that he gave in the last months of his life, Hani placed great emphasis on the importance of moral values, tracing his own to three sources: his religious upbringing, the non-racism and love of democracy that he acquired through the ANC and the SACP, and his education in classical and English literature. While he was in his second year at Fort Hare the ANC was banned after the Sharpeville massacre and he came under the influence of Govan Mbeki, father of Thabo, who wrote extensively on the Transkei, as well as of Raymond Mhlaba, later commander of Umkhonto we Sizwe (MK), and Andrew Masondo, a Mathematics lecturer. Hani was drawn into a socialist study group and read the *Communist Manifesto*, noting its religious language, and Emile Burns's *What is Marxism?*, a political primer by a Scottish communist, which was much used by the British and South African communist parties. He joined an underground SACP cell at Fort Hare in 1961, seeing no contradiction between that and continued church attendance.

It was his interest in the Catholic Church, as well as the possibility of becoming a lawyer, that led him to the study of Latin, and he also did Classical Studies, reading the Greek classics in translation. He was fascinated by the Roman historian Tacitus's *Histories* and was 'moved beyond words' by the plays of Sophocles and Euripides. He read and re-read Homer's *Iliad* and *Odyssey*, noting the relevance for exiles of Odysseus's struggle to regain his kingdom. He enjoyed tracing the links between

21

these Greek authors, English poets like Chaucer and Dryden, and religious writing. Bringing the various ethical strands together, he said: 'The Greek tragedies can be seen as an ancient form of contextual theology, an attempt to relate the common ethical ideals of society to the contemporary issues of the day. The classical tales were a serious quest for human values. Religion is a quest for spiritual fulfilment and moral perfection. Political struggle is about the creation of a better world in which to live. They are for me all facets of a multi-faceted quest for human completion. Intellectuals have a special obligation to make the insights of former ages available for the present struggle. They can assist us not to make the same mistakes and to forge models of human existence based on the wisdom of the past.'

2

Armed struggle

The turn to armed struggle had been under discussion
within the ANC and the SACP since the early 1950s, but
it was only after the Sharpeville massacre and the banning
of the ANC in 1960 that there was a move from abstract
discussion towards action. Leading members of the ANC,
such as Chief Albert Luthuli, and of the SACP, such as
Moses Kotane, had doubts about this course of action.
Around the middle of 1961 a decision was made by both
organisations to found Umkhonto we Sizwe (MK) as an
autonomous organisation. It was formally established
in July 1961 and launched a sabotage campaign on 16
December of that year. Soon afterwards, in January 1962,
Nelson Mandela left South Africa to travel through Africa
and to Europe, seeking financial and logistical support,
military training for MK recruits, and weapons.

After completing his degree at the end of 1961 – he
graduated at Rhodes University, which gave degrees for
Fort Hare, in April 1962 – Chris Hani moved to Cape
Town to join his father, who was determined that he

should become a lawyer. He wanted him to be 'a black Sam Kahn', referring to the communist lawyer and Cape Town city councillor, who was a member of parliament for the Western Cape as a representative of so-called 'Native' interests from 1949 to 1952. Hani was articled to a firm of attorneys in Cape Town. Through his father's connections, and the links that he had established at Lovedale and Fort Hare, he was rapidly co-opted onto the underground regional committee of the ANC, also known as the Committee of Seven. He also worked with the ANC-aligned South African Congress of Trade Unions (SACTU), which remained a legal organisation. In the course of 1962, he joined MK and at the end of the year he underwent military training with other recruits under Denis Goldberg on a farm at Mamre, near Cape Town.

He had no real difficulty in reconciling his turn to armed struggle with his religious convictions, but he had difficulty in understanding the opposition of the churches in South Africa to it. 'Still under the influence of the Church, I was disturbed and challenged by the open hostility of Church leaders to armed struggle. They were downright insensitive to black frustrations and despair and narrow in their understanding of violence and who was responsible for it. I realised that the Church had throughout history condoned a defensive military action as well as providing theological justification for the right of the oppressed to resort to military action to remove a tyrant. "So what the hell was going on?" I asked.'

He had, meanwhile, been arrested with Archie Sibeko and another man in possession of ANC leaflets against the proposed 90-day detention law and was sentenced to 18 months in prison. They were defended by Albie Sachs, who succeeded in getting them released on bail pending an appeal. While on bail, Hani may, according to one source, have attended the meeting held at Lobatse in Bechuanaland between internal and exiled members of the ANC in October 1962, though he does not refer to this in his own recorded recollections. He certainly did attend the fifth conference of the SACP, held secretly in Johannesburg in 1962, which adopted a new programme, *The Road to South African Freedom*. There he met leading members of the SACP for the first time, including its long-serving general secretary, Moses Kotane, and Walter Sisulu, who had joined in 1955. When the appeal against the prison sentence failed, Govan Mbeki, who was a member of the high command of MK, decided that there was no point in Hani and Sibeko going to prison. They should go underground to avoid arrest and then travel abroad for military training.

In May 1963 Hani and Sibeko moved north to Johannesburg, where they joined up with a group of 28 MK recruits who were being assembled to travel to Tanganyika via the Bechuanaland Protectorate and Northern Rhodesia, which was still part of the settler-controlled Federation of Rhodesia and Nyasaland. Martin Thembisile Hani then adopted the *nom de guerre*, or MK name, by which he was usually known in his early years in exile, choosing the first two names, Christopher Nkosana, of one of his brothers. He later dropped Nkosana, but retained Chris, while resuming his original surname.

The party was led by Mark Shope, a leading member of SACTU. They were met at the Lobatse border with Bechuanaland by Joe Modise, later commander-in-chief of MK, who had family links with the protectorate and played an important role in the smuggling of people out of the country. They travelled north by truck, using the track between Francistown and Kazungula on the Zambezi where four countries, Botswana, Namibia, Zambia and Zimbabwe, meet. This enabled them to avoid travelling through Southern Rhodesia, where a group, including Thabo Mbeki, had been arrested and turned back in the previous year. They expected the ANC's representative in Lusaka, Sam Masemola, to meet them on the Northern Rhodesian/Zambian side of the border, but he failed to arrive. They crossed over on their own on 20 May and spent the day hiding in the bush. Eventually Shope went on alone to Livingstone and returned with a truck. Seeing that the police were out in force at Livingstone railway station, apparently on the lookout for them, they joined the train at Zimba, 80 kilometres north of Livingstone.

Immigration officials boarded the train at Kafue, 50 kilometres south of Lusaka, and detained some members of the party. Others were detained by officials who met the train in Lusaka, but some, including Hani, who had managed to borrow a baby to sit on his lap, and Shope, who was able to pass as a Zambian, evaded detention. They were taken to the homes in Lusaka of leading members of the United National Independence Party (UNIP) and the Northern Rhodesian ANC, which had recently formed a coalition government, though the country remained under the overall control of the British colonial governor.

Some of the detained members of the group managed to escape from the immigration authorities, while others, including Sibeko, were eventually released after a successful habeas corpus application. UNIP and the Northern Rhodesian ANC organised transport to take the released men, and those who had earlier evaded arrest or escaped from detention, to the Tanganyika border. From there they travelled north by bus to Mbeya and then by train to Dar es Salaam. Tanganyika was the first independent African country that they had visited, and the exiled leaders of the ANC, including Oliver Tambo and Duma Nokwe, were then based in Dar es Salaam. Hani and other members of the party met them there for the first time and were also introduced to Tanganyika's leader, Julius Nyerere. Hani was impressed by Tambo's solicitude for the new arrivals.

They stayed only three months in Tanganyika before moving on to the Soviet Union where Hani and other potential leaders of MK, and organisers of the underground, were trained near Moscow. Many other recruits were sent for more conventional military training at Odessa in the Ukraine. It was originally intended that Hani's group should be in the Soviet Union for only six months, but their stay was extended to a year and they did not return to Tanganyika until August 1964. Hani recalled that his military training course included theories of guerrilla warfare, and training in underground work, as well as more conventional topics such as topography, firearms, military engineering, and the manufacture and use of explosives. Hani thought that the military training was useful and well suited to their needs, but it was the political education, and the social and cultural experience of the Soviet Union, that had the greatest impact on him and his group, confirming their commitment to socialism.

Coming from a deeply racist society, they encountered 'a new world of equality, of people where our colour seems to be of no consequence and where our humanity is being recognised'. They travelled widely in the Soviet Union, visiting Leningrad (now St Petersburg) and Tashkent in Uzbekistan. They were exposed for the first time to ballet and to classical music. They visited museums and learned about the history of the Russian Revolution, 'when power actually was taken from the hands of the rich few ... the people coming into the streets and seizing the properties of the few ... So we were actually eating and lapping [up] all this information ... that was hidden from us in this country. We had never read anything like that before in this country [South Africa]. So our appetites were really whetted. They were sharpened by this new experience.'

It may also have been at this time that Hani was first exposed to the writing of the Russian and Soviet novelist Maxim Gorky. His descriptions of peasant life had a strong resonance and a lasting impact on Hani, who later recalled: 'Gorki's writings have a certain religious aura to them. They portray the cultural and spiritual adhesion, the religious centre, that binds a peasant people together in exploitation, sustaining them from one generation to the next. Gorki understood the hardness of peasant life, rebelling against the conditions that condemned large sections of the population to a life of squalor and human degradation, while condemning the intelligentsia who had lost their sense of the heroic. He realised that intellectuals, and let me say many politicians, are distant from peasant reality, even when seeking to be most supportive of the poor.'

On their return to Tanganyika, Hani and the other members of the group were met by Oliver Tambo, who impressed on them the urgent need for them to get back to South Africa to help to rebuild the shattered underground. The Rivonia arrests and the trial, resulting in the sentencing of Mandela, Sisulu, Govan Mbeki, and other ANC leaders to life imprisonment, had taken place since their departure from South Africa. Meanwhile they were sent to Kongwa, near Dodoma, to set up a camp. Hani was appointed political commissar of the camp, which meant that he had responsibility for the political education and morale of the MK members there. There was only one building on the site and they lived in tents until they were able to put up more structures. Inspired by the self-help philosophy of Julius Nyerere, they also engaged in farming, growing crops, and raising chickens and pigs. Land had been set aside at Kongwa by the Tanganyikan government, through the Liberation Committee of the newly established Organisation of African Unity (OAU), for other Southern African liberation movements. It was here that members of MK became friendly with members of the Zimbabwe African People's Union (ZAPU). This was, within a few years, to have significant consequences with the formation of an informal alliance.

Hani was disappointed that the SACP was not organised and had no presence in Africa outside South Africa. He met Moses Kotane in Dar es Salaam, both before and after his journey to the Soviet Union, but the party was never mentioned. He even met Kotane in the Soviet Union, but still there was no mention of the party. He was probably then unaware that a decision had been made, following Nelson Mandela's tour of East Africa in 1962, to downplay the ANC–SACP alliance in Africa. This was because of the hostility towards communism of Nyerere and Kenneth Kaunda, the leaders of the countries that were to become Tanzania and Zambia, and the ANC's most significant hosts. The SACP was not permitted to organise within the ANC in Africa – a decision that had the support of leading members of the SACP in the region, Moses Kotane and J.B. Marks, and it remained in force until 1969. Hani thought that this was unfortunate as it made it difficult to deal with the tensions, reflecting the Sino-Soviet split, that emerged at Kongwa between MK cadres who had been trained in the Soviet Union and those trained in China. Later on, he was to be disappointed that there was no message of support from the SACP to the participants in the Wankie Campaign.

Hani did not stay long at Kongwa. By June or July 1965 he had moved south to Lusaka in Zambia, which had become independent in October of the previous year. The first official representative of the ANC in Zambia was Thomas Nkobi, later national treasurer of the organisation, who arrived early in 1964, but he was replaced in January 1965 by Tennyson Makiwane, a journalist, who had been transferred from London. Nkobi remained in Lusaka as deputy representative and was restored to his position as chief representative after the temporary departure of Makiwane in 1969. By mid-1965 the ANC's official representation had grown to six members. As 'administrative secretary', Hani, using the name Chris Nkosana, ranked third after Makiwane and Nkobi. The other three representatives were Memory Miya, a SACTU official, Ulysses Modise, publicity secretary, and Johannes Tau-Tau. Hani was a rising star in both the ANC and MK. He played a significant role over the next two years as administrative secretary, and, from mid-1966 onwards, as secretary of the committee that was set up to organise the return home of trained military personnel.

Although he was later critical of class distinctions within the ANC in exile, Hani was at this stage a beneficiary of them. The senior officials, Makiwane and Nkobi, were paid £45 a month. He received £35 a month, as did Michael Dingake, who was based in Bechuanaland and paid from the Lusaka office, but Modise and Tau-Tau received only £8 a month.

From the moment that Zambia attained its independence, Oliver Tambo and other leaders of the ANC in exile, including Duma Nokwe, the secretary-general, began to work on President Kaunda and other members of the new government to get permission for the movement of trained military personnel, and military material, through the country. By the second half of 1965 there were a few MK men in Lusaka – often referred to in letters and accounts as 'students', 'boys' or 'mates'. Some of these may have been in transit southwards and were kept in a house in the township of Lilanda, or on a small-holding at Kaluwa's, east of Lusaka. Unlike the officials, they received no salary, but accommodation, food and a small cash allowance.

Apart from liaison with the Zambian government, the main activity of the ANC officials in Lusaka related to the maintenance of communications between South Africa and the headquarters in Tanganyika (which became Tanzania in December 1964) through Bechuanaland.

The key link in the chain was Michael Dingake who spent most of 1965 rebuilding lines of communication in Bechuanaland. His arrest, while travelling through Rhodesia by train in December 1965, shortly after UDI (Rhodesia's unilateral declaration of independence), and his subsequent transfer for trial and imprisonment in South Africa, was a calamity, as he was the man with the best knowledge of the internal underground. Hani spent much of his time travelling between Lusaka and Livingstone, where he was engaged in reconnaissance for crossing points to Bechuanaland and Rhodesia on behalf of the committee for getting MK men 'home'. Other members of the committee included Lambert Moloi, who was later an MK commander in Lesotho. Hani recalled that on one occasion he was arrested in Bechuanaland, detained for two weeks, and then sent back to Zambia as a prohibited immigrant. He was also responsible for the dispersal and concealment of arms and ammunition, which were brought in from Tanzania, sometimes with, and sometimes without, the knowledge of the Zambian government. Archie Sibeko was responsible for the movement of the arms across the border.

In the course of 1966 Joe Modise, MK's commander-in-chief, a small number of MK men, and two or three women, moved south from Kongwa to Lusaka. The attitude of the Zambian government to the presence of MK was ambivalent. Some of its members were arrested and sent back to Tanzania and others had to lead an underground existence, coming out only at night, for most of a year. The ANC hoped that the independence of Bechuanaland, as Botswana, in September 1966 would open up communications with South Africa. The new government of Seretse Khama, operating with the advice of British officials, was, however, determined not to jeopardise its relationship with its powerful neighbour, South Africa, by permitting the ANC to use the country as a base or for the transit of MK personnel. The effective closing down of Botswana led to increased interest in cooperation with ZAPU and the use of Rhodesia as a route to South Africa.

3

The Wankie Campaign

Chris Hani was an enthusiastic advocate of the alliance with ZAPU and the use of the Rhodesian route. Although it may have been discussed in 1966, it was probably only in March–April 1967 that an informal alliance was formed and that plans began to be made for a joint expedition across the Zambezi into Rhodesia. These plans were confirmed at a meeting of the ANC's National Executive Committee (NEC) in Lusaka in June 1967 after serious debate. Moses Mabhida, the political commissar of MK, was one of those who were doubtful about the proposal. He was not opposed to the alliance in principle, but to the strategy of sending men across the Zambezi in large groups. Other members of the military headquarters, including Mavuso Msimang and Peter Tladi (also known as Lawrence Phokanoka), spoke strongly against the proposed strategy, doubting that it was sound in terms of the established principles of guerrilla warfare as no reconnaissance work had been done across the river, and no political work had been

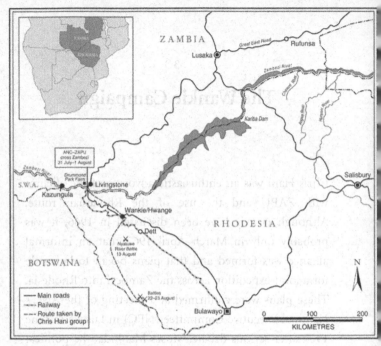

The Wankie campaign

carried out with the prospective host population. There
was an assumption, which turned out to be ill-founded,
that ZAPU members knew the terrain and could relate
to the local population. Some leaders of ZAPU also had
reservations about the proposed alliance, fearing that it
would provide South Africa with an excuse for military
intervention in Rhodesia. In the end it was the insistent
demand for action from the MK cadres at Kongwa – there

had already been desertions to Kenya – that overcame the doubts of some members of the leadership.

According to Hani, the ANC's plan was to set up the infrastructure for a 'Ho Chi Minh trail' through Rhodesia to South Africa, bypassing Botswana. He emphasised that Oliver Tambo was highly supportive and actively involved in the preparations for this expedition. He recalled that a hand-picked group of ANC and ZAPU cadres did physical, political and military training near Livingstone for over three months – between April and July 1967. Hani was one of only two members of the ANC's planning committee who volunteered for action – the other was Lennox Lagu, who became the ANC commander. The overall commander was John Dube from ZAPU and Hani was appointed the ANC's political commissar, effectively the ANC's second-in-command.

The party was intended to cross the Zambezi in the fourth week of July, but Chief Albert Luthuli died on 21 July and the crossing was delayed until after his funeral. In commemoration of 'the Chief', Oliver Tambo gave the name 'Luthuli Combat Detachment' to the MK group, which comprised about 50 of the 79 men who crossed the Zambezi at the Batoka Gorge, about 24 kilometres south of the Victoria Falls, on the night of 31 July, and during the following day. Oliver Tambo, Thomas Nkobi, and Joe Modise were present at the river crossing as were the ZAPU commanders, including Dumiso Dabengwa. Nkobi recalled that Hani was the first man across and that he could be seen on the far bank doing exercises. He told one of the men waiting to cross the river, who acknowledged his fear, that everyone feels fear, but the thing to do is to learn how to overcome it. Pointing to Hani, he said: 'You see that man there also has fear but he can suppress his and conquer it. That's what he's doing as you see him jumping.'

Although it was written nearly 20 years after the events that it describes, Hani's own account is the best by a participant of what became known as the Wankie Campaign. He was not the most senior commander of MK and ZAPU – he was only 25 years old at the time – but he was one of the most articulate of them, and his reactions to these events were to have a major impact on the ANC as a whole. A focus on Hani may make him appear to be the hero of the campaign, but, in reality, there were many heroes and almost all the participants, whether from the ANC or ZAPU, displayed great courage.

According to Hani, who is said to have set a brisk pace, morale was high and there was 'a spirit of elation and joy' when they crossed the Zambezi. They soon, however, ran into unanticipated problems. Although they crossed the river in the dry season, they had expected that they would find streams with water flowing towards it. They soon found that the terrain was very dry, and that the few people who lived there were dependent on boreholes. The shortage of water, and then of food, forced them to make contact with the local population sooner than they had hoped would be necessary. Hani acknowledged that this was dangerous as they might have encountered people who were hostile to them or working for the government. He says, however, that they were well received and this does seem to have been the case. The Rhodesian security forces became aware that a guerrilla detachment had entered the country about a week after it crossed the river. They did not find this out from local informers, but from the interrogation of stragglers. As many as ten men were unable to keep up the pace and became separated from the main force in the first two weeks after they crossed the Zambezi.

The plan was that the detachment should split into two groups when it reached the Wankie game reserve. One group of about 21 men, most of whom were members of ZAPU, was to move east towards Lupane and the Nkai Reserve, where they would establish a base to service future contingents passing through to the south. The second group of about 48 men, most of whom were from MK, though there was also an escort of ZAPU members who were to act as guides and interpreters, was to move southwards towards South Africa and to establish MK units inside the country. As well as Hani, this group included John Dube, the overall commander, and Lennox Lagu, the MK commander. Hani was himself the leader of a unit of from six to eight men, which was intended to reach Cape Town. Other units were expected to reach the Transkei, Durban, and the northern Transvaal.

It was the smaller, eastern group that first made contact with Rhodesian forces two weeks after they had crossed the Zambezi. They had noticed that spotter planes were searching for them, and they had an encounter with members of the Rhodesian African Rifles on the dry riverbed of the Nyatuwe River on 13 August. Four or five MK members were killed or died of wounds following this first clash, but their comrades fought back and killed at least two members of the Rhodesian forces and injured others in a long gun battle. As a result of a further clash on 18 August, 14 of the remaining 15 members of the eastern group were killed or captured. The overall casualty rate for this group was very high, but individual members of MK, including James Masimini, who refused to leave his post though severely wounded, fought back with great courage. In a separate incident on 16 August, Basil February, who had a special mission to travel south by train ahead of the main detachment, was killed in a shoot-out on a farm near Figtree on the Botswana border.

After what Hani described as this 'premature' engagement with the enemy, aerial surveillance was stepped up and his party became aware that spotter planes were searching for it. They found that there was much less bush cover than they had expected and they took to marching at night in small groups with scouts and outliers. Every morning they scattered in a defensive circle and dug themselves into shallow trenches and foxholes. They had no two-way radios and were unable to communicate with Lusaka, but they did have a transistor radio and heard Rhodesian news reports of the clashes with the eastern group. They realised that they would soon see action and looked forward to this as an opportunity to put their training into practice. They also became aware that the South African government had sent in forces to back up the Rhodesian army and police.

Their first clash with the Rhodesian forces came on the evening of 22 August, three weeks after the detachment crossed the Zambezi. Conscious of their lack of ammunition and supplies – they were limited to the contents of their knapsacks, and were unable to obtain fresh supplies of ammunition or reinforcements – the members of the detachment had resolved not to fire until they could see their enemies. They did not immediately respond to a hail of bullets from their opponents. When they did reply it was with considerable effect. They inflicted casualties on the Rhodesian forces who withdrew, abandoning food, weapons, including a light machine gun, and a two-way radio. Hani's estimate of the Rhodesian forces killed, which he put at from 12 to 15, was probably exaggerated, but they did lose at least two dead, including a white officer and a black sergeant-major, and had several wounded. Hani's group lost three dead and one wounded. They saw this as a memorable victory and knew that there was no going back: 'despite all these odds, fighting away with no back-up from HQ actually with no communication from HQ, there was never a feeling that: "*Guys, we are in trouble now, the enemy has attacked us. Let us run back to Lusaka.*" We were moving and nothing was going to stop us. We moved on after having that fantastic feast. We proceeded because it could have been dangerous just to celebrate and wait there. We knew the enemy was going to organise reinforcements. But I think we had imparted to the enemy or conveyed an important message, namely that "*we are not just push-overs, you enemy must know that we are a serious fighting force*".

Hani recalled that the next battle came a week later, but it seems to have come on the following day and followed an aerial bombardment by jet aircraft of an area about two kilometres away from the detachment's actual encampment. On this occasion, on 23 August, the overall commander, John Dube, decided that they should go on the offensive for the first time.

Hani recalled: 'We organised units to go and raid the enemy. I was in that together with James April, Douglas Wana, the late Jack Simelane, Victor Dlamini and others. We crawled towards the enemy's position and first attacked their tents with grenades and then followed with our AKs and L[ight]M[achine]G[un]s. The enemy fought back furiously and after fifteen minutes we called for reinforcements from the rear, and within ten minutes we overran the enemy's position.'

The Rhodesians were again forced to abandon their positions and equipment, losing several dead and wounded. Hani saw this as a victory and emphasised that 'the Luthuli Detachment was never defeated in battle'. After this incident the southern group broke up into several smaller groups. They were short of food and water, under intense aerial surveillance, and moving through difficult terrain with Rhodesian forces in hot pursuit, and decided to withdraw into Botswana. They did so with a view to rest and recuperation before proceeding on their way southwards and had no intention of surrendering to Botswana's paramilitary police, but they found themselves chased into Botswana by Rhodesian and South African forces. At the same time Botswana was under pressure from South Africa to stop them entering the country. They made what Hani described as 'the correct political decision' that they would not fight with the Botswana paramilitary, and so surrendered to them. He says that they were given an assurance that they would not be detained, but they were arrested. They were charged and sentenced to varying terms of imprisonment, depending on whether they were found with or without weapons. The first group, led by Hani, entered Botswana on 27 August and further groups crossed the border in the vicinity of Plumtree, about 500 kilometres south of their starting place, on 3 and 4 September. By that time about two-thirds of the original members of the southern group had entered Botswana.

Hani rejected the views of contemporary critics who saw the Wankie Campaign as an example of adventurism or desperation. He maintained that 'it would have been wrong for us to wait for a favourable situation in terms of some rear bases or some country bordering South Africa getting independence. It was important for us to rough it and to participate in creating favourable conditions for ourselves. That is what a revolutionary is and that is what revolutions are about.' Writing in 1986, he saw the Wankie Campaign as inspiring the post-1976 generation and claimed: 'The ANC and MK continues along that old path opened by the Wankie Detachment.'

Hani was understandably proud of the courage displayed and the sacrifices made by his comrades in the Luthuli Detachment. It is difficult, however, to avoid the conclusion that the Wankie Campaign was a heroic failure. Casualties were high and the objective of establishing a trail or corridor through Rhodesia to South Africa was not achieved. There are no precise figures, but it seems likely that about 30 members of the original group of 79 were killed in action or died of wounds, about 20 were captured in Rhodesia, and about 30 took refuge in Botswana. One man got back to Zambia; one man, who either was or became a policeman, got back to South Africa, and one man passed through South Africa to Swaziland.

The Rhodesian forces lost seven or eight dead and about 15 wounded in what they called 'Operation Nickel'.

The figures for casualties may seem unbalanced, but most of the Rhodesians who were wounded received medical treatment and survived, while most of the members of the Luthuli Detachment who were wounded in action died on the battlefield. Some of the highest praise for the performance of the detachment came from their Rhodesian opponents. The long-serving head of Rhodesia's (and Zimbabwe's) Central Intelligence Organisation, Ken Flower, recalled that the Rhodesian 'commanders in the field reported that the guerrillas' morale and standard of training was much higher than anything yet encountered in Rhodesia; the guerrillas had fought a military action face to face, with no civilians involved, and were defeated only by the Security Forces' air power, mobility, and much greater effectiveness in communications and medical services.' The Rhodesian Selous Scouts commander, Ron Reid-Daly, considered the Rhodesian army's actions in the Wankie and later Sipolilo campaigns – Operations Nickel and Cauldron – to be 'the most significant operations of the war'.

Speaking to Wolfie Kodesh shortly before his death, Hani acknowledged that the Wankie Campaign failed to achieve its objectives militarily speaking, but he said that it was 'an important experience for us as individuals. We tasted military action. WE were tempered in battle. WE were tested in difficult conditions and I think we succeeded ... We did succeed, we inspired people. The press in SA which was quiet now talked about the ANC fighting battles in Zimbabwe. The media told the people that the ANC was *kaput* but here it was fighting.' There was a resurgence of black political activity. 'This was a reawakening in the country.'

In an interview in 1991 Hani said: 'Looking back we can see that the Wankie Campaign was the beginning of incipient armed propaganda. An important feature of Wankie was that it delivered a message: MK was still alive. The spirit of resistance was alive ... It was no accident that the Black Consciousness Movement was launched inside the country at that time. I believe it was inspired to some extent by the 1967 Wankie Campaign.'

4

After Wankie and Sipolilo
The Hani Memorandum

Chris Hani was sentenced to an effective two years in prison in Botswana for entering the country carrying weapons of war. As a result of pressure from the OAU and the intervention of President Kaunda of Zambia with President Khama on the occasion of his state visit to Botswana in May 1968, it was agreed that ANC and ZAPU prisoners would be released after serving a year of their sentences. Hani and some other members of the Luthuli Detachment were repatriated to Zambia in September 1968.* Although he was unhappy about his arrest and detention, he had no real complaints about his treatment in Gaborone Maximum Security Prison. The people of Botswana were generally sympathetic. Hard labour involved work in the prison gardens, watering plants, and there was plenty of time to read books, which

---

* Some sources say that Hani returned to Zambia in December 1968, but James April is certain that it was in September.

were sent in by people outside. He continued his duties as political commissar, taking responsibility for the morale of his fellow MK prisoners.

While Hani and his comrades were in prison, the ANC and ZAPU launched a second expedition into Rhodesia – the Sipolilo Campaign. They had learned some lessons from the Wankie Campaign. Instead of sending men into Rhodesia with only weapons, ammunition and food that they could carry, with no radio communications and no possibility of reinforcement or replenishment, a chain of small base camps was established on the south side of the Zambezi between December 1967 and March 1968. There was continuous movement across the river and members of the leadership of both organisations, including Joe Modise and Dumiso Dabengwa, spent time on the south side of the river in the sparsely populated Sipolilo game reserve. It was only in March that the Rhodesian forces became aware of the ANC–ZAPU presence and that clashes took place. Some members of the detachment were able to get back to Zambia while others moved deeper into Rhodesia and were either killed or captured there. It is likely that rather more men were deployed in the Sipolilo Campaign than in the Wankie Campaign and that similar numbers were either killed or taken prisoner in the two campaigns. Leonard Pitso, one of the participants in the Sipolilo Campaign, and a surviving signatory of the Hani Memorandum, believes that 'the cream of MK' was lost during the latter campaign.

On his return to Lusaka, Hani and his comrades found that there was a singular lack of interest on the part of the ANC and MK leadership in the 'heroes and martyrs' of the campaigns and in the lessons to be learned from the survivors. The returnees were shocked by the lack of any kind of official welcome by the leadership and by its failure to debrief them with a view to learning the lessons of the campaign. Sometime in 1970 Hani – 'Comrade Chris' – told an internal commission of inquiry into later incidents in Lusaka that 'after leaving prison in Botswana he found the Movement in a *stalemate position. There was no longer any direction, there was general confusion or an unwillingness to discuss the lessons of the revolution*'.

Hani's role in the Wankie Campaign gave him a reputation for physical courage. His role in the aftermath of the campaign gave him a reputation for moral courage. He was by no means the only hero of the Wankie and Sipolilo campaigns and he was not the sole author or signatory of the trenchant memorandum that came to bear his name. Leonard Pitso insists that it was a collective effort and he is a little doubtful about the way in which it has come to be identified with one man, as is Mavuso Msimang. Hani was the primary signatory, but there was input into it by all the signatories, and by people who did not themselves sign. The choice of who would sign, and the placing of Hani's name at the top, were in themselves political acts. But there is no doubt at all that Hani displayed courage in allowing his name to be put forward as the leader of the group and that this was the result of a sense of deep frustration and anger. The other signatories were Leonard Pitso, Jackson Mlenze, Robert Mbanjwa, Wilmot Hempe, Alfred Khombisa and Ntabenkosi Fipaza. Hani and Mlenze had returned from Botswana after the Wankie Campaign and three signatories, Pitso, Mbanjwa and Fipaza, had taken part in the Sipolilo Campaign.

Pitso is clear about the background to the memorandum – dissatisfaction with the ANC–ZAPU alliance and with Rhodesia as a route to South Africa, as well as unhappiness about the inability of the leadership of the ANC in Lusaka and Morogoro, Tanzania, whether political or military, to recognise publicly the sacrifices made by the 'heroes and martyrs' of Wankie and Sipolilo, to welcome and to debrief the prisoners on their return from Botswana, or to engage in any real analysis of the lessons to be learned from the campaigns. The leadership seemed to be embarrassed by the losses and unable to face the survivors and come to terms with what had happened.

Pitso recalls: 'We asked what guarantees were there that ZAPU if it won would provide the ANC with a base? There was no real alliance – nothing in writing. What were we going to say to the families of those who were killed? What were they fighting for? After Wankie and Sipolilo there was no analysis, no announcement of deaths in action, no commemoration of heroes and martyrs. We knew that inside South Africa the underground was completely broken down. We knew that there were sell-outs in the NEC ... The NEC was itself divided and there was a division between the ANC and MK ... We wanted the NEC to sit down and analyse Wankie and Sipolilo. What happened? What were the mistakes? We wanted concentration on the home front, not international solidarity. We wanted a conference to establish proper structures, to hold elections, to confirm Tambo in place ... We wanted a new direction and to look forward ...'

Hani himself recalled his state of mind after his return from Botswana and the official reaction: 'I didn't think that there was an interest in our experience and what we had done and what was the next step. We stayed there literally waiting ... And we waited ... We were in that state of limbo, state of suspense. And I and others could not stomach it. We blurted out. We blew our tops. And some leaders got angry. I think people generally were not used to be criticised. They thought we were just going to applaud everything they did, and say, hallelujah. I think the leadership at that time was not ready to get criticism from underlings, from subordinates. And some of them blew their tops and wanted us to get punished. And we were punished in the sense that for some time we were left in the cold.'

The 3,000-word document, which was probably written in January 1969, and which became known as the Hani Memorandum, opened with the statement:

'The A.N.C. in Exile is in a deep crisis as a result of which a rot has set in. From informal discussions with the revolutionary members of M.K. we have inferred that they have lost all confidence in the A.N.C. leadership abroad. This they say openly and in fact show it.' The authors of the memorandum went on to protest that ordinary members of the ANC had been neither represented at, nor consulted or informed about, several recent conferences involving the leadership. They suggested that members of MK were no longer recognised as members of the ANC. They referred to the 'disintegration' of MK and the 'careerism' of the ANC's leaders abroad. They pointed out that there had been no attempt to send leaders home since the Rivonia arrests and that more effort was needed to reach the masses 'in the language of our people'. They objected to the payment of salaries to senior ANC officials, to the commander-in-chief of MK, Joe Modise, and the chief political officer. They objected to Modise's purchase of an expensive car and about double standards on health provision – senior leaders were sent abroad for medical treatment. They objected to the 'fossilisation' of the leadership and to a small number of people carrying out a multiplicity of roles, and demanded its renewal and rejuvenation. They said that the leaders abroad had become 'professional politicians not professional revolutionaries', and demanded equal treatment for all in the ANC and MK, as well as the selection of cadres on merit.

They accused the ANC's leadership of becoming a 'middle class' of 'globetrotting' and salaried bureaucrats who had created 'a machinery which has become an end unto itself', and which was increasingly divorced from 'the home front'. They said that MK had become independent of the political organisation; that there was conflict between the ANC and MK; and that the ANC had lost control over MK. They blamed the NEC for allowing the commander-in-chief, Thabo More (Joe Modise), to run MK singlehandedly and arbitrarily. They also accused Modise of a preoccupation with the running of 'mysterious business enterprises', namely a furniture factory in Lusaka and a bone meal factory in Livingstone, in conjunction with 'dubious characters with shady political backgrounds' – they doubted whether 'with his attention so divided he can do justice to the armed struggle in South Africa which should be his primary and absolute concern'.

They were also scathing in their criticism of the security department, then under the control of Duma Nokwe, the secretary-general. They saw it as internally directed and 'doing nothing against the enemy' – it had not even been able to determine the fate of cadres missing in 'Zimbabwe'. It had, however, 'become notorious. Those who serve in it have the central task of suppressing and persecuting genuinely dedicated cadres of M.K. who have nothing to lose by participating in the struggle but their chains!' They also referred to 'secret trials and secret executions' and to the 'emergence of extremely reactionary methods of punishment in M.K'.

They protested that there had been no 'comradely reception' for the returnees from Botswana and 'criminal neglect of our most dedicated comrades who have fallen in battle' and of those who had been sentenced to death or to long terms of imprisonment in Rhodesia. They asked: 'How can we possibly keep quiet about these valorous sons of South Africa?' They listed the names of many of those who had been killed in action or taken prisoner and accused the leadership of 'callousness and irresponsibility' – of 'complete indifference and apathy to the heroes and martyrs of our Revolution who have fallen in South Africa and Zimbabwe'.

They contrasted their treatment with the favours accorded to the leaders' sons who were sent to European universities and 'who are being groomed for leadership positions after the M.K. cadres have overthrown the fascists and will just come home when everything has been made secure and comfortable for them'. They took particular exception to the appointment of Thabo Mbeki as a leader of what they described as a 'bogus' ANC youth organisation.

Above all they regretted the failure of the leadership to provide an opportunity for the analysis of the lessons of the Wankie and Sipolilo campaigns with a view to the development of 'strategy and tactics', and a proper definition of the 'form and content' of the ANC–ZAPU alliance. The signatories demanded a renewal of the leadership and concluded with a demand that 'all these problems must be resolved by a conference between the ANC leadership and members of M.K., and not just handpicked individuals'.

According to a second memorandum, an appeal against their expulsion from the ANC – and there is no doubt that they were expelled, not just suspended – which was written by Hani and the other signatories with the help of Jack Simons in March 1969, they had not originally intended to write a memorandum at all. They had delegated three of their number to interview Duma Nokwe 'with a view to arranging a discussion with members of the Executive'. Nokwe 'took up a hostile attitude, maintained that the issues we had raised were trivial, and proposed to interview us individually and not as a group. We considered this procedure to be unpolitical and refused to comply.' Nokwe offended them by failing to recognise Jackson Mlenze, a Wankie veteran and a member of the deputation. They, on the other hand, infuriated Nokwe by their suggestion, repeated in the memorandum, that Amiran, an Israeli agricultural equipment company, for which his wife, Vuyiswa (Tiny), was then working, was a front for Israeli intelligence – Shin Bet. Nokwe 'told our representatives to arrange a meeting with members of the Executive'. The delegates then prepared a statement for presentation to a meeting with six members of the NEC. This became the memorandum, which was then 'typed, stencilled and duplicated' in the ANC office. Copies were provided to members of the executive and to 'selected members of MK', who were all advised to treat the matter as highly confidential.

At their next meeting with the executive the signatories were shocked to find that members of the military headquarters and regional administration were present. They were told that these men had been called in because the memorandum had been circulated to members of MK. The signatories wanted a discussion of the political content of the memorandum, while the leadership of MK who were present threatened to 'deal with them' for alleged violations of the MK oath. The chairman rejected their view and closed the meeting indefinitely.

According to Hani and the other signatories, orders were then given for their arrest for alleged treachery. Dungeons or trenches were dug on the ANC farm at Livingstone for their incarceration. Oliver Tambo, the acting president, ordered these to be filled in and called a general meeting of members at ZAPU's Joshua Nkomo camp near Lusaka to consider the matter. Eyewitness accounts of this meeting, which took place in February 1969, agree that Tambo defused the situation by taking personal responsibility for the failings of the ANC leadership. But he also suggested that the signatories were being used by other members of the leadership 'as brooms by which the leadership swept its dirt'. According to Joe Matthews, then a member of the national executive, it was on this occasion that Tambo acceded to one of the memorandum's main demands when he announced the calling of the Morogoro Conference, which took place at the end of April.

The signatories were suspended and then summoned to appear before a tribunal consisting of five members, two of whom were members of the NEC and three of whom were members of the military command. They protested that they could not get a fair trial from a tribunal that included members of the NEC, which was the main target of their critique, and at least one member of the regional military headquarters who had shown bias against them. They refused to appear before the tribunal and were expelled from the ANC in Lusaka on 25 March 1969. Their expulsion was confirmed by the ANC 'headquarters', presumably the National Working Committee, on 29 March 1969.

The appeal document may not, however, tell the whole story. Chris Hani told Vladimir Shubin, a Soviet official and good friend of the ANC, in 1992 that the majority of the members of the tribunal voted for 'the most severe punishment', a euphemism for the death penalty, and it was only the determined intervention of Mzwai Piliso, later head of the security department, that 'averted what would have been a tragedy'. It was widely believed in exile that Hani and the other signatories were sentenced to death, but there is no evidence to confirm this and the balance of probability suggests that they were not. There is no doubt, however, that 'dungeons', 'trenches' or 'graves' were dug for their incarceration, or burial, at Livingstone and that these were filled in on the instructions of Oliver Tambo. Major-General Sandi Sijake recalls that he and Lambert Moloi found 11 freshly dug and empty 'graves' on the ANC farm there and suggests that some members of the military leadership had more than the seven signatories marked down for execution.

Whether or not it was linked to the tribunal, there does seem to have been a plan to imprison, and possibly kill, Hani and the other signatories. Hani was staying at this time with Livingstone Mqotsi, a leading intellectual from the Eastern Cape and an expelled member of the Unity Movement. He recalled that Hani thanked him for saving his life after he denied entry to his house to a group of MK men who came looking for him at midnight. Ray Simons recalled that Govan 'Dingo' Hashe, an MK member who was usually based on the Livingstone farm, came to tell her that there was a plan to kill Hani. In the absence of Tambo, she warned Thomas Nkobi, who had replaced Tennyson Makiwane as chief representative, of the dire consequences that would follow should anything happen to Hani. Surprisingly for a life-long communist, she told him that 'it would not be like the communist countries' – in other words, there would be publicity. She would herself tell the whole world.

On his return to Lusaka, Tambo asked for a meeting

with the signatories, which took place at the house of Jack and Ray Simons. Jack Simons chaired the meeting, which was attended by 30 or 40 people, including Tennyson Makiwane. Tambo was, according to Pitso, 'very friendly' and showed that he had a good understanding of what the signatories had been saying. He did not think that they had been trying to break up the ANC. The NEC was, however, split on the issue and there could be no immediate reinstatement.

Looking back over 40 years, Leonard Pitso acknowledges that the signatories may have made some mistakes. It may have been unduly provocative to name names and to make personal attacks on Joe Modise, on Duma Nokwe and his wife, Tiny, on Thabo Mbeki, or, by implication, on Moses Kotane. It may also have been a mistake to circulate the memorandum to embassies. He believes that Jeqe Buthelezi (Mbanjwa) passed it to the Chinese embassy, and a version without the names found its way to the Soviet embassy. But Pitso still believes that the memorandum was on the right track. 'The memo was a strategic document. We wanted a debate within the NEC to take things forward. We wanted the mass democratic movement to be mobilised. The Strategy and Tactics document [which emerged from the Morogoro Conference] mentioned political preparation, but it did not happen. It was not until after the visit of Tambo, Slovo and others to Vietnam in 1978 that the ANC took mass mobilisation seriously. The formation of the UDF followed from that and after that everything changed for the better ... If the memorandum had been taken seriously and the lessons of Wankie and Sipolilo learned then, this could have happened ten years earlier. There was a need to build the mass democratic movement – and a front of all forces against apartheid.'

5

The Morogoro Conference
and after

Hani had no doubt, and there really can be no doubt, that the memorandum was the main catalyst for the calling of the Morogoro Conference. As a result of their expulsion neither Hani nor any of the other signatories could be present at the conference. The memorandum was not debated at the conference, but it cast a long shadow over the proceedings. A probable majority of the 80 or so delegates present at the conference were from MK and many of the issues raised in the memorandum were discussed. The most important result of the conference was the opening of the ANC in exile to whites, coloureds and Indians, bringing it into line with the multi-racial membership of MK. Although this had not been mentioned in the memorandum, it had, according to Leonard Pitso, been a matter of concern. There can be no doubt that the main pressure for this important change came from within MK. It amounted to the abandonment of the multi-racial Congress

Alliance as it had existed in the 1950s and a step towards non-racialism.

Tambo offered his resignation during the proceedings, but was persuaded to return to the acting presidency. The NEC was reconstituted by a troika of Tambo, Kotane and Marks, and Duma Nokwe lost his position as secretary-general. Joe Modise lost the title of commander-in-chief, though he continued as commander of MK, and was promoted to membership of the new Revolutionary Council. This was set up to strengthen political control of MK and to allow whites, such as Joe Slovo, Indians, such as Yusuf Dadoo, and coloureds, such as Reg September, to assume leadership roles.

The conference also adopted a new 'Strategy and Tactics' document, which had been drafted by Joe Slovo with some input from Joe Matthews and Duma Nokwe. In a concession to the demands of the memorandum, it conceded that revolutionary armed struggle was a form of political struggle and insisted that 'our movement must reject all manifestations of militarism ... The primacy of the political leadership is unchallenged and supreme and all revolutionary formations and levels (whether armed or not) are subordinate to the leadership.'

In the latter months of his life Chris Hani was certain that the conference was an important turning point: 'after Morogoro we never looked back'. He thought that the 'Strategy and Tactics' document became the 'lodestar' of the movement and the establishment of the Revolutionary

Council led to a new emphasis on political work and the development of the underground. It was, however, only five years later that geopolitical changes following the coup in Portugal and the movement towards independence of Mozambique and Angola, made it possible to revive the underground, something with which Hani was himself to be closely involved. It was almost ten years before the new emphasis on political work began to be implemented. Tambo seemed to be reluctant to challenge Modise's militarism and this may have been the result of a provincial conflict with ethnic undertones – the Cape versus the Transvaal – which had its roots in the reaction within MK to the Hani Memorandum and which broke out in Lusaka soon after the conference.

Although the Hani Memorandum was not specifically discussed at the conference, it recommended that the question of an amnesty and the reinstatement of the signatories should be referred to the newly reconstituted NEC. They were reinstated in June when Hani and Hempe were restored to the commissariat and Mlenze was made a member of the Lusaka staff command. It was this, taken together with what appeared to be Modise's effective demotion, which led to the outbreak of conflict within MK in Lusaka. Although Pitso was Sotho-speaking and came from Cape Town, all the other signatories of the memorandum were Xhosa-speaking and came from the Eastern Cape and the Transkei. They came to be known to some as the Cape group. Their reinstatement and the promotion of three of them provoked a backlash from the Transvaal 'comrades', who refused to take orders from the new Lusaka staff command. After a meeting with Tambo during which they voiced their grievances, Hani, Hempe and Mlenze volunteered to step down, but their offer did not solve the disciplinary problems in Lusaka, which continued for another year or so.

These problems were compounded by pressure from the Zambian and Tanzanian governments, which had promoted the Lusaka Manifesto. This was signed by all but one of the East and Central African states at a meeting in Lusaka in April. It indicated a desire to step back from confrontation with South Africa, which was seen as an independent state, and to emphasise and prioritise the anti-colonial struggles of Angola, Mozambique, Zimbabwe and Namibia. Hani was himself very critical of the Lusaka Manifesto, but he realised that the ANC was in no position to attack its hosts. Within a few months the remaining members of the MK contingent at Kongwa had to be airlifted to the Soviet Union and an additional 60 MK cadres were also sent there for further training in order to reduce the tension in Lusaka. In 1970, 30 MK members were expelled from the ANC in Lusaka as a result of their refusal to move to a bush camp during the Non-Aligned Conference.

At about the same time Hani was mentioned as a possible member of a small group of men led by the ANC's political commissar, Flag Boshielo, a member of the NEC, which set off for South Africa via the Namibian Caprivi Strip in August 1970. Boshielo and his three companions, two of them Wankie veterans, vanished without trace, but were believed to have been betrayed by the paddlers who took them across the Zambezi and killed by South African forces, who had a presence in the Caprivi Strip. It is not certain that Hani was part of the plan, which had Tambo's reluctant acquiescence, but, if so, he dropped out and escaped death. He travelled with Tambo, Joe Modise and John Motshabi to investigate the scene of the disappearance, but they came up with no positive information. It showed some magnanimity on Hani's part to travel with Modise, who had, allegedly, wanted him dead only a year or so previously. But, whatever the tensions there were between them, they were able to work together pragmatically for a further 20 years.

In retrospect Chris Hani thought that Oliver Tambo dealt well with the aftermath of the memorandum. 'He moved away from punitive vindictive action to understanding what is primary in building our organisation ... not just to be punishing people who criticised our movement.' Hani thought that this was the culture of the ANC which it should take forward into the future and he gave Tambo credit for eschewing the cult of personality and welding a team – 'one of his most important and immortal contributions'.

That was his retrospective view, as recorded shortly before his death, but there is no doubt that Hani, who was

65

normally a buoyant and exuberant person, went through a period of deep depression after his return from Botswana. After the crisis over the memorandum, the threat to his life, and his expulsion from the ANC, he withdrew for a while to the Copperbelt, where he stayed with expatriate friends. He seems to have contemplated leaving the ANC, returning to legal studies, and looking for a career outside the movement. His friends James April, also a Wankie veteran, and Archie Sibeko were among those who visited him in the Copperbelt and who sought to persuade him to return, which he eventually did.

He was also appreciative of the support of Jack and Ray Simons in his time of 'isolation', and for the more remote support of leaders of the SACP, Yusuf Dadoo and Joe Slovo. Jack Simons not only chaired the meeting with Tambo, and helped draft the appeal, but also ran political education classes at his home for the benefit of those who had been expelled. These continued after their reinstatement and were open to other members of MK. They discussed theoretical issues and also more practical questions like how to rebuild the underground and how to work within 'reactionary' institutions such as Bantustans and urban councils. It was only at a meeting between representatives of the ANC and the SACP after the Morogoro Conference that the SACP was given formal permission to organise in Tanzania and Zambia, though not within MK, which was in any case then in disarray. Hani told Sonia Bunting that he had disagreed with Moses Kotane's opposition to the organisation of the SACP in Africa and was actively involved with Ray Simons and others in the setting up of party units in Lusaka from 1969 onwards. Jack Simons was not then a member of the SACP and did not join until the late 1970s. The SACP's central committee had its first meeting in Africa in Dar es Salaam in 1971. Hani was either appointed or elected assistant general secretary of the SACP in 1972, at a time when the substantive general secretary was still Moses Kotane, who had been incapacitated by a stroke at the end of 1968 and was living in a clinic in Moscow.

* * *

Several documents survive from the early 1970s in which Hani expressed his views on the situation in South Africa, especially the areas that he knew best, the Transkei and the Western Cape. He had two major preoccupations, as did the ANC itself: how to respond to the evolution of the apartheid regime's Bantustan policy and the move of the Transkei from nominal self-government towards 'independence'; and how to react to the emergence of the Black Consciousness Movement, which had first appeared among black university students in the late 1960s under the leadership of Steve Biko and others. This drew largely on black American sources, and on black theology, but also on the writings of people like Frantz Fanon. It was the first new political movement to appear in South Africa since the suppression of the ANC and its allies in the early 1960s. The leading Black Consciousness organisations included SASO (the South African Students' Organisation), founded in 1969, and the BPC (the Black People's Convention), founded in 1971. In the early 1970s they were receiving more international support from countries like Sweden than was the ANC in exile.

At a meeting of the ANC's information and research committee in May 1970, which was attended by Thomas Nkobi, Jack and Ray Simons, and Duma Nokwe, among others, Hani led a discussion of the Bantustans. He called for a reassessment of the ANC's approach to work within the Bantustans and a clearer definition of the movement's basic tactics. He said that the Transkei Democratic Party was setting the pace in opposition to the system and he called for the ANC to explore the possibility of participation within it: 'above all we should provide the answer to the question as to whether our people still reject or accept the concept of independence through Bantustans'.

A year later he was the co-signatory with Sizakele Sigxashe of a document submitted to the Revolutionary Council on 'internal reconstruction' in the Cape. They indicated that there had been contact within the last year with people in the Libode, Flagstaff and Matatiele districts of the Transkei who had been prepared to receive MK people sent in from outside. They also had three independent contacts in the Western Cape, but thought that people should not be sent there directly for political or military operations, but rather by way of the Ciskei or Transkei. They had no firm contacts with the Eastern Cape and Border regions (Port Elizabeth and East London). They were aware of student unrest in secondary schools in the Transkei and thought 'that this youth will be the backbone of the armed struggle'. It was important to send people into the area to provide political and military leadership.

They were also aware of the growth of Black Power in the colleges and universities – they saw this as 'an illustration of black anger and frustration', which was taking the form 'of bitterness and non-cooperation with the enemy but no positive confrontation'. They needed to have people on the spot 'to provide guidance and leadership by telling the people that there is a solution – maximum mobilization and armed struggle'. They thought that it should be made compulsory for all members of the ANC in exile to study and understand these new trends and developments – there was 'a serious, regrettable political deterioration in our ranks abroad'. If this was not stopped there would be very few people on the outside who would be able 'to cope with leadership responsibilities in the country'. They argued that the survival of the ANC abroad depended on 'the revival of political study groups, the main purpose of which will be the preparation of a self-sufficient cadre, capable of taking decisions in line with general ANC policy'.

Perhaps the most important, and as it turned out prophetic, part of their paper was the suggestion that internal reconstruction and propaganda work 'could be carried out illegally in countries that are hostile to us'. The countries they mentioned included Botswana, Lesotho and Swaziland. They suggested that 'our most disciplined and dedicated cadres should be instructed to take up illegal work' in these areas. Operations there 'would be a wonderful school of revolutionary work' and would prepare 'our men ... to tackle the most arduous tasks in S[outh] A[frica]'. Three years later, in what turned out to be a brilliant move, Oliver Tambo sent Hani and Thabo Mbeki, who were certainly among 'our most disciplined and dedicated cadres', to Lesotho, Botswana and Swaziland to begin the work of internal reconstruction and propaganda.

In November 1973 Hani, using notepaper with the letterhead of the ANC's Algerian office, but apparently writing from Moscow, sent instructions to Ray Simons in Lusaka to pass on to 'Mildred' (or 'Milly'), apparently an emissary from the Transkei. She should organise people to infiltrate both the major political parties in the Transkei, Matanzima's Transkei National Party and Knowledge Guzana's Transkei Democratic Party, in order to promote the ANC's programme. Among other things they should press for the expropriation of white-owned farms in the Transkei, and of the rich, the abolition of the pass laws, the extension of trade union rights, an end to the state of emergency in the Transkei, and the building of more hospitals and health centres.

During the early 1970s Chris Hani also began to play a diplomatic role. In November 1972 he visited Sweden under the name Zenzile Msethu and attended the conference at Gothenburg of the Swedish Liberal Party, a party which was to the right of the Social Democratic Party, but a consistent supporter of the ANC from the 1960s. At that time he also had a meeting with officials of the Swedish foreign ministry and briefed them on the situation in South Africa. In April 1973 he returned to Scandinavia under the same assumed name for the UN–OAU conference which was held in Oslo. In the following week he again visited the Swedish foreign ministry. He began to establish close ties with Sweden and with the Swedish aid organisation SIDA. These were reinforced when he became the ANC's chief representative in Lesotho in 1976 and was involved in negotiations with SIDA for humanitarian aid for the ANC in that country.

*Joe Slovo, Chris Hani and Joe Modise at the celebration of the
75th anniversary of the ANC, Lusaka, 8 January 1987.
(Photo: Mayibuye Centre)*

6

Interlude in Lesotho, 1975–82

About the middle of 1974 Hani began preparations to enter South Africa to re-establish the underground there. He spent three months in the German Democratic Republic where he did training in underground work with Joe Slovo, who recalled that the original plan for his infiltration involved the use of a bicycle. It was only rather late in the day that Hani acknowledged that he was unable to ride a bicycle and needed a 'crash' course.

Shortly before his departure for South Africa, Hani married, in Lusaka, Limpho (pronounced Dimpho) Sekamane, a citizen of Lesotho, who had been doing a course at the Mindolo Ecumenical Centre at Kitwe on the Copperbelt. Her father had been a leading member of the Pan Africanist Congress (PAC)-aligned Basutoland Congress Party (BCP). She had no connections with the ANC, but had been a member of the BCP, and her brother became a leader of its armed wing, the Lesotho Liberation Army, which was set up in the late 1970s with South African government support. It is not clear when

Chris met her, but they had both had earlier relationships. Hani was involved in 1965–66 with a British teacher in Lusaka with whom he remained in contact until the end of his life.

Hani crossed the Botswana border into South Africa using false papers in September 1974 and travelled by train from Zeerust to Johannesburg. He stayed for a few weeks – he says weeks but others say months – with relatives in Moroka (Rockville) Township in Soweto. He could not stay longer because of the harsh penalties that had been introduced for people found harbouring 'terrorists'. He moved on to Lesotho, where his father had been settled with Elizabeth Mafikeng since 1963 at Mafeteng. They ran a café there – its patrons included the lawyer and former ANC Youth League, and PAC, leader, A.P. Mda. His son, the novelist Zakes Mda, claims that Hani, known to him as 'Bhut' Thembi' (Brother Thembisile), sometimes helped him with his Latin homework. Gilbert Hani and Elizabeth Mafikeng, known locally as 'Fiks', were among the founders of a small ANC branch in Lesotho, which was set up in the early 1970s when there were only a few ANC refugees in the country.

Hani was able to use these family connections to establish himself in Lesotho. He found that Lambert Moloi, another MK commander, also known as 'Comrade A', was already there, as were Fanele Mbali (also known as Lemmy Booi), leader of the failed 'Operation J', an MK plan to land cadres on the coast of Pondoland, and

Mathabatha Peter Sexwale, brother of Tokyo Sexwale. The government of Chief Leabua Jonathan, which had refused to accept defeat by the BCP in the elections in 1970 and had effectively seized power in a coup, was not then very well disposed towards the ANC, and for two years Hani and Moloi led an underground existence with no permanent home. Initially they had no money, but they were able to make contact with Joe Slovo, who sent funds from London. Hani sometimes travelled into the Transkei for meetings, while others from their 'collective' travelled to Cape Town, Durban and Johannesburg. They began the work of re-establishing the ANC's underground networks in the Western Cape, the Eastern Cape and the Free State, something that Thabo Mbeki, Albert Dhlomo and Stanley Mabizela were doing at the same time in the Transvaal and Natal from Swaziland. Hani and Mbeki were both elected to the ANC's NEC in 1974 at the age of 32, becoming the committee's youngest members.

Sometime in the middle of 1975 Hani and Moloi were arrested, detained for 90 days, tortured and deported to Mozambique, but they were soon able to return to the country. Chief Jonathan had suspected them of providing support to the BCP. Later in the year Hani became the ANC's officially recognised chief representative, when Jonathan turned against the South African government, suspecting it of support for the opposition. Limpho Hani, who had been studying in Yugoslavia, returned to Lesotho at the end of 1975 and they were later able to set up home there, staying at first in a house that came to be called 'Moscow' in a suburb of Maseru.

After the Soweto Uprising in 1976 there was an influx of young refugees into Lesotho as there was into Botswana and Swaziland. Many of them were recruited by the ANC and had to be transferred overland to Swaziland for onward transmission to Mozambique. Limpho Hani was involved in the ferrying of recruits across South Africa to Swaziland. She was herself detained in South Africa in 1977–78 and was held for several months. While a prisoner, she gave evidence for the state in a case against Mountain Qumbela, a former leader of the ANC in the Western Cape.

Thenjiwe Mtintso, a former student at Fort Hare, went into exile in Lesotho in 1978 and was recruited to the ANC and the SACP by Hani, as was her partner, Skenjana Roji. She credited Hani with a better understanding of the philosophy of Black Consciousness than she had herself. 'It was the first time that I was introduced seriously to the notions of socialism and communism. It was not just in the theoretical sense but in giving meaning to my own life as a worker. In the Black Consciousness Movement we believed "you are Black first, before you are anything," so there wasn't a class content, there wasn't a gender content. After meeting Hani, I began to understand the relationship between class, race and gender.'

Hani was proud of the liaison work that he did in the late 1970s and early 1980s on behalf of the ANC with established trade unions like the Food and Canning Workers' Union, and with emerging black trade unions, and the Federation of South African Trade Unions (FOSATU), as well as with the Black Consciousness Movement and black civic organisations, such as the Port Elizabeth Black Civic Organisation (PEBCO). According to Jeremy Seekings, many of the civic organisations that were set up in the Eastern Cape and Border regions were inspired by Chris Hani and the ANC in Lesotho. Another source says that members of a committee in Lesotho, including Hani, Moloi and Skenjana Roji, were responsible for this.

In an interview after Hani's death, Joe Slovo, who was MK's chief of staff in the late 1970s and early 1980s, emphasised that Hani's primary role in Lesotho was political, not military. He may have been involved in recruitment and some training for MK, but for reasons of geopolitics, and the vulnerability of Lesotho, all military operations were organised from outside. In fact there was almost no MK action in the Cape in the time that Hani was in Lesotho. Almost all MK activity in South Africa in these years took place in Natal and the Transvaal, and was organised from Swaziland. According to the ANC's evidence to the Truth and Reconciliation Commission (TRC), there were no MK operations in the Western Cape and only two or three attacks on railway lines in the Eastern Cape between 1978 and 1982. There were also one or two assassinations, including that of Tennyson Makiwane, the leader of the so-called 'Gang of Eight', who was then working for the Transkei Bantustan, in Umtata in 1980. An MK member, David Simelane, claimed amnesty for the murder of Makiwane from the TRC in 1997, but it is not clear who, if anyone, in the ANC gave the orders for this action, which was repudiated by Oliver Tambo.

In its evidence to the ANC's Politico-Military Strategy Commission in 1978, the Lesotho collective, in which Hani's was the leading voice, made it clear that 'We have always felt that political work is primary and that everything else flows from it'. They had made it compulsory for all MK members to start with political organisation before carrying out any military tasks. They emphasised the importance of the political underground for providing protection, shelter and intelligence to MK operatives. They had established a system of autonomous sectors, each with its head. Some of the heads were based in Lesotho and visited their sectors in South Africa. Some were based in the Transkei and visited Lesotho to report. They had also set up intelligence and propaganda units.

They emphasised the importance for mass mobilisation of working with legal and semi-legal organisations. They had made discreet contacts with the opposition Democratic Party in the Transkei and were interested in making contact with the coloured Labour Party and with non-racial sporting bodies like the South African Rugby Union (SARU). It was in this context that Hani had contact with white radicals, including the four rugby-playing Watson brothers from Port Elizabeth. According to Daniel 'Cheeky' Watson, Hani took over the mentorship of the four brothers in 1978–79. 'Gavin and I would stay in the country and Valence and Ronny would move on supposedly buying trips ... They would ... have all the discussions in Lesotho and ... then come back.'

Howard Barrell, a journalist who went on to write about the history of MK, recalls that on a visit to Lesotho in 1978 he offered to distribute leaflets on behalf of the ANC. Hani's response demonstrated something for which he was well known – his concern with people's psychological readiness and commitment. He accepted Barrell's offer, but suggested that he take a month to think about it. When Barrell returned and said that he felt he was not yet ready, Hani told him that his decision showed a mature awareness of his limitations. Years later, after Barrell had done leaflet and intelligence-gathering work for other ANC commanders, he went into exile. Hani then told him that his hesitation had convinced him that, if he did change his mind, he would probably be able to trust him.

Vusi Pikoli, later director of public prosecutions, who became involved in radical politics through SARU, went from Port Elizabeth with others to Maseru in 1980 with the intention of joining the ANC and going for military training. They met Hani, who told them that they would not be sent abroad – they should stay in Lesotho to help

79

with the strengthening of the underground in the Eastern Cape. They were given some basic military training, as well as training in intelligence work, in Lesotho, staying in the country until they were expelled in 1986. Pikoli and others studied at the university while doing underground work. He was eventually sent via Lusaka for three months' military training in Angola, but this was not until long after Hani's departure from the country.

The relationships between ANC exiles in Lesotho were not always harmonious. There was evidently some tension between Hani and Moloi, with some people suggesting that they led rival 'factions'. Moloi was born in Lesotho and was very close to Joe Modise, so it is possible that these tensions reflected long-standing rivalries within MK dating back to Kongwa Camp and the Wankie Campaign. Thozamile Botha, a founder of PEBCO, went into exile in Lesotho in 1980, but had a difficult relationship with Hani, and a more difficult one with Limpho, whom some people described as prickly, before moving on to Zambia.

Life in Lesotho became increasingly dangerous for Hani and his family. He survived an attempt on his life in 1980, when his car was damaged, and another attempt in 1981, when the person planting a bomb under his car was seriously injured. It was characteristic of him that he took care of the injured man, who later escaped while on bail and returned to South Africa. In the same year, Vusi Pikoli's friend Sizwe Kondile was abducted from Lesotho with Hani's car, which was found abandoned near the Swaziland border. There were suspicions that Kondile might have become an agent, an askari. It was only in 1990 that Dirk Coetzee, in evidence to the Harms Commission in London, gave information about his abduction, torture, and murder near Komatipoort. His body was burnt and his remains were thrown into the Komati River. Hani had been among those who thought that Kondile had been 'turned', and Limpho Hani was allegedly rude to some of his comrades. In a gesture of reconciliation, shortly before his own death, Hani told Kondile's mother that he would be prepared to speak at a memorial service for him.

The ANC withdrew Hani from Lesotho for the first time early in 1981 and then again in 1982. On the latter occasion the Lesotho government asked for his removal, saying that it was not safe for him to stay in the country. He spent time in Lusaka and Maputo, but visited his family in Lesotho in October. His wife and children narrowly escaped death in the South African raid on Maseru in December 1982 when 15 South African special operations units – a total of about 80 men – attacked houses and flats in and around the town. Thirty members of the ANC, including Hani's successor as chief representative, Zola Nqini, and many women and children, were killed in the raid, together with a dozen Lesotho citizens. Limpho Hani left the country for a while and stayed in Maputo, but she returned at the end of 1984 and was employed there by SIDA from 1985 to 1987, and by the Swedish embassy from 1987 to 1989. Leabua Jonathan was overthrown in a South African-backed military coup in 1986 and Lesotho ceased to be a useful base for the ANC and MK. Limpho Hani left Lesotho with her children in 1989 and was reunited with her husband in South Africa in 1990.

7

Political commissar
Zambia, Angola, Mozambique

Chris Hani was appointed deputy commander and commissar of MK in 1983 on the establishment of the Military Headquarters (MHQ) in Lusaka. In these capacities he ranked number three in the MK hierarchy after Tambo, commander-in-chief, and Joe Modise, army commander, and ahead of Joe Slovo, chief of staff, and his friend and rival, Lambert Moloi, who was chief of operations. From 1982 to 1984 Hani's time was divided fairly evenly between Lusaka, Angola, where most members of MK were based in camps, and Maputo. He stayed in Maputo with Albie Sachs, a friend from Cape Town days, as did his family when they arrived from Maseru after the South African raid in December 1982. He worked very closely with Joe Slovo and the special operations team that was based there.

Hani emphasised that, as commissar, he was responsible for political education and morale. He had to contend with serious problems of morale in the Angolan camps, which he visited for the first time in 1981, and where he spent a good deal of time in 1983. These problems stemmed primarily from the isolation of the camps and their residents from the frontline and their location in a country that was a major target of South African destabilisation and racked by civil war. Tanzania and Zambia would have been much more suitable places, but neither country was prepared to allow the ANC to set up camps for the military training of the young people who left South Africa after the Soweto Uprising in 1976. The leaders of MK, including Modise, Slovo and Hani himself, spent most of their time in Lusaka or Maputo, and the commanders in Angola preferred to spend their time in the capital city, Luanda. The situation in the Angolan camps had never been good, but deteriorated after the South African air raid on Novo Catengue in 1979 and the *Shishita* crisis in 1981, when an alleged spy ring was discovered. The provision of food, education and entertainment was inadequate and medical services were almost non-existent in areas where malaria was endemic. A further problem was the brutality of the security department, sometimes called Mbokodo, the grinding stone, which was staffed by young and inexperienced men with little or no political education.

Slovo and Hani were the senior leaders of MK who retained the respect and affection of the men, and the few women, in the Angolan camps. They both showed some understanding of the predicament of people who wanted to get into action in South Africa, but were often stranded in the camps for years on end because the ANC lacked an underground apparatus in South Africa strong enough to receive them, and the resources to get them there. As commanders who were themselves involved with operations, they also offered people in the camps the prospect of getting into action. Hani inspired loyalty through his ability to remember the names and histories of all the people who had passed through Lesotho, and his genuine interest in people as individuals. Neither Mzwai Piliso, head of security from 1981, nor Andrew Masondo, the national commissar, the two senior MK officers in Angola in the early 1980s, had his interpersonal skills. When Oliver Tambo asked for suggestions in 1982 for the reorganisation of MK, they threatened to discipline people in the camps who came up with critical responses.

The first of the Angolan mutinies happened in January 1984 and followed the loss of MK cadres who were fighting alongside the Angolan army – FAPLA – against Jonas Savimbi's UNITA forces on the Kwanza River in the north-eastern part of the country. Hani recognised the need for this involvement, as communications between Luanda and the camps in the north had been made difficult by ambushes, and thought that it was necessary for MK to defend its camps and its position in Angola. He was personally involved in the fighting alongside FAPLA against UNITA, but he was not in Angola at the end of 1983 when MK sustained a number of casualties in ambushes in the Kwanza River area. He was on holiday with his family in the Soviet Union when MK cadres returned from the front to camps north of Luanda. He was in Angola in mid-January 1984 and met some of the mutineers there. They had a number of demands: that they should be sent into action in South Africa; that the security department should be suspended; that the Quatro (Camp 32) prison camp should be investigated; and that Tambo, who was in the country, should address them. Hani undertook to pass on the demands to Tambo and the NEC, but there was no immediate response. By early February the focus of the mutiny had shifted to Viana. As Hani recalled, they 'took their weapons, they took trucks and they virtually took over our transit camp in Viana, in Luanda'. They were asking: 'Look, we are dying in Angola, why are we here, why are we fighting here and not fighting at home?' Hani, who, while travelling with Joe Modise, survived a grenade attack at this time, addressed a meeting with the mutineers, who had been encouraged to elect their own representative Committee of Ten.

According to his later account, the mutineers then refused to desist and 'we had to appeal to the Angolans to come, to help us disarm them'. They were disarmed and were then sent back to the camps. The Committee of Ten had negotiated this disarmament, but soon afterwards its members were arrested, with about 20 others, and sent to prison in Luanda. About 300 other mutineers were moved to camps at Pango and Quibaxe, north of Luanda. Hani was initially sympathetic with many of the mutineers' complaints, but he lost sympathy with them when they became violent. Some of the mutineers recalled him saying: 'You are pushing us down the cliff. You are stabbing us in the back.' Hani thought of the mutiny as 'counter-revolutionary', and he came to see it as inspired by enemy agents.

This was not the conclusion of the members of the ANC's Stuart Commission, named after its chairman, James Stuart (MK name of Hermanus Loots), which investigated the mutiny over a three-week period in February–March 1984. It concluded that there were sufficient real grievances to explain the mutiny without recourse to conspiracy theories. There had been a growing division between the administration, including the security apparatus, and the rank-and-file members, with hugely differential access to food, cigarettes and liquor. The division was so extreme that some people spoke of there being two armies, an imperialist army led by Andrew Masondo and Mzwai Piliso and a revolutionary army led by Slovo and Hani. The commission described 'a nearly total collapse of the political, military and moral organisation' in Angola, with resultant 'confusion, fear and lawlessness'. It suggested that the 'People's army' seemed to be placed on 'the lowest, or nearly the lowest rung' of the movement's priorities. The commission suggested that the solution to the problems in Angola was not punitive discipline, but political work, without which, it accurately predicted, there would be another mutiny. It said that people might think that the situation was under control, but 'the fires had been doused, not extinguished'. It recommended the release of the prisoners held in Luanda, an amnesty for the Committee of Ten, and the calling of a consultative conference, which had become the mutineers' main demand. The prisoners were not then released, but the conference was called and took place a year later at Kabwe in Zambia.

Hani returned to Maputo after the quelling of the Viana mutiny. He was in Maputo at the time of the announcement of the Nkomati Accord, a non-aggression pact between South Africa and Mozambique, on 16 March 1984. As a result of this the ANC was reduced to a diplomatic mission. Many leaders of the ANC, including Slovo and Hani, were banned from the country, and as many as 160 MK cadres, and many other ANC members, had to leave. Hani was involved with others in sending MK cadres through Swaziland to South Africa. Many of them were rounded up and deported from Swaziland to Zambia – others got through to South Africa, but few of them survived underground for long.

The second, more serious mutiny broke out at Pango in May. There is little doubt that the Nkomati Accord was a factor in provoking it, as MK cadres who were deeply frustrated by their inability to get into action in South Africa saw the main route through Mozambique and

Swaziland being closed down. Hani later recalled that he was in favour of negotiations with the mutineers, but 'I reached the end of my tether when they killed several key commanders in one camp called Bango [Pango], and took over the camp. We had no alternative but to go and capture the camp and reassert authority.' Similar numbers of people were killed on both sides. Hani deeply regretted the loss of life: 'Very sad because these were all members of the ANC, fellow South Africans.' Hani was not a member of the tribunal that was set up to try the leaders of the mutiny – he may, indeed, have declined to participate in it. Sixteen of the mutineers were sentenced to death and seven were publicly executed immediately by a firing squad. It was later acknowledged by several ANC leaders that they had no proper legal defence. Some sources say that Gertrude Shope, a leader of the ANC's Women's Section, intervened to stop the executions, but Hani recalled: 'I rushed back to Lusaka and said to the leadership: Stop the executions ... do anything, sentence them, but don't execute them.' He later told Ronnie Kasrils: 'These mutineers behaved savagely. When we saw how they had slain some of our people in cold blood I was as mad as the rest of us. After seven were executed and I thought of another twenty awaiting the firing squad – some I'd known as young recruits in Lesotho who had clearly been misled – I felt we must stop. I appealed to Tambo in Lusaka over the heads of the local commanders who were determined to press on with the verdict of the tribunal.' Tim Mokoena, the commander who had led the suppression of the mutiny, was apparently annoyed by Hani's intervention, but later conceded that he had been right.

Hani was not in Angola in the latter part of 1984, but he visited Quatro, the prison camp where the surviving mutineers were held, in February 1985. He was clearly shocked by the conditions there and he raised the matter at meetings of the NEC in 1985, 1986 and 1987, risking opprobrium by doing so. In an unusual criticism of Oliver Tambo, he said that he was too slow to act about Quatro and about the excesses of the security department, which was eventually reorganised in 1987, when Joe Nhlanhla replaced Mzwai Piliso as its head. There was, however, no great improvement in its performance and there was continuing tension with MHQ.

The mutinies in Angola continued to haunt Hani and, in the view of some critics, they are his weakest link. Although he had campaigned in the NEC for the reform of Quatro, and was, according to Vladimir Shubin, regarded as 'a bit of a softie' on matters of detention and interrogation, he continued to believe that some, but not all, of the mutineers were agents acting on behalf of the South African government. In his last speech as MK chief of staff in August 1991, he referred to the '1983 mutiny' and the continuously deteriorating security situation that MK had faced in Angola throughout its stay in the country until its departure in 1989. He claimed then that there was general agreement that it had been right to crush the mutiny, but that the ANC had failed to explain 'the unfortunate events' surrounding it. It was then necessary to do this in order to 'neutralise Mwezi Twala and his band of counter-revolutionaries' – a reference to the campaign that was being waged against the ANC by the Returned Exiles Coordinating Committee (RECC), a group of former Quatro detainees, who were acting, according to Hani, with the support of the security police and a right-wing American pressure group. In December 1989 he had been sent with Stanley Mabizela to Tanzania by the NEC to enforce a resolution that former mutineers, including Twala, should not be allowed to sit on the Regional Political Committee to which they had been elected. Although there is no evidence to support the allegation, Hani has also been held responsible by some for the murder by MK members in the Transkei in 1990 of another former Quatro detainee, Sipho Phungulwa, who had been one of his bodyguards.

There is no way of proving or disproving allegations of this kind, but it is curious that Hani, who was one of the sternest critics within the ANC leadership of the security apparatus and its excesses, should be blamed for them. Joe Slovo remarked in a filmed interview after Hani's death: 'It is a calumny and slander to place him in the same category as some of those people who were responsible for some of the abuses of human rights.' There was continuous tension between MK and the security department from 1981 onwards. This came to a head following the death, soon after his release from a period in solitary confinement in Lusaka, in November 1989, of Muziwakhe Ngwenya, known as Thami Zulu, or TZ, a Natal commander of MK. Neither Hani nor any of the senior commanders of MK believed that he was an enemy agent, as had been alleged. Suspicion fell on him because of heavy losses as a result of the ambush of MK groups crossing the border into South Africa from Swaziland. Hani demanded that a commission should be set up to investigate the circumstances of his death, the reasons for his isolation, and why he was not released until he was on the point of death. He said that the military leadership had consistently raised the question of detention. Torture could be psychological as well as physical. 'We are on the verge of power and need to be seen to value human rights.' He had the support at this time of other MK commanders including Joe Modise and Ronnie Kasrils, head of military intelligence.

In an interview that he gave shortly before his death, Hani was sceptical about the absorption of people who had served the apartheid regime into a new security service. But there were equally, he said, people within the ANC 'who I would oppose as part of a new security force. I have my own experience. I know my own movement, I know their roles and their attitudes, and I would like a situation where a security apparatus is answerable to parliament.' He insisted that never again should unchecked powers be given to the security apparatus and he rejected any refusal by officials to answer questions on the grounds of national security.

He concluded: 'The security must not hide behind the president or the prime minister and refuse to be accountable to parliament and to the public. I'm aware of the fact that elements of the ANC, PAC and government will serve in a new security apparatus, but there must be clear guidelines to avoid the sort of thing that happened to a very small extent in the ANC and to a very large extent within the security forces of the regime.'

Hani (seated next to Cyril Ramphosa) on a flight from Lusaka to Dar es Salaam after Mandela's first visit to the Zambian capital in March 1990. (Photo: Rashid Lombard)

8

From people's war
to negotiations

There is no reference to 'people's war' in the ANC's
'Strategy and Tactics' document of 1969. It seems probable
that this phrase first appeared in the 'Green Book', the
report of the Politico-Military Strategy Commission,
which was drawn up after the visit of ANC leaders,
including Tambo, Slovo and Modise, to Vietnam in 1978.
Chris Hani was not a member of the commission, and did
not take part in the debates that accompanied it, but the
report included, as has been shown, a document from the
Lesotho collective, of which he was the leading member.

The report posed the question: 'Do we see the seizure
of power as a result of a general all-round *nation-wide
insurrection*, which a period of armed struggle will have
helped to stimulate; or are we embarked on a *protracted
people's war* in which partial and general uprising will
play a vital role?' It opted for the latter formulation,
and on the relationship between political and military
struggle it concluded: 'At the present moment we are at

the stage where the main task is to concentrate on political mobilisation and organisation so as to build up political revolutionary bases in the country. In as much as the growth of the armed struggle depends on the rate of the advance of the political struggle [it] is secondary at this time.'

Reflecting the advice of the Vietnamese strategist Colonel Giáp, it concluded that the main purposes of armed struggle were:

'a) to keep alive the perspective of People's revolutionary violence as the ultimate weapon for the seizure of power.

'b) to concentrate on armed propaganda, that is, armed action whose immediate purpose is to support and stimulate political activity and organisation rather than to hit at the enemy.'

It was really only in his role as political commissar of MK from 1983 that Hani began to make public statements about military strategy. According to Mac Maharaj, no mean strategist himself, Hani and Joe Slovo were the main military thinkers in the ANC, but Hani did not leave much of a paper trail in the currently open archives, nor was he, despite his literary education, a prolific writer of articles. He was, however, a highly articulate interviewee, and interviews are the main source for his views on political and military developments in the 1980s.

In his emphasis on the political control of MK, on the need for a strong underground, and on the primary importance of political work, Hani was totally consistent from the time of the 1969 memorandum onwards. In a lecture that he gave in the camps in Angola in 1983 on mass mobilisation he stressed the importance of the emergence of independent trade unions and the need for them to recognise the 'indivisibility and interconnection of the economic and political struggle'. At the same time he emphasised 'the need to deepen our influence in civic, student and intellectual organisations'. As for the role of the military itself, he said: 'Building a People's Army in order to fight a people's war actually means that our movement and our army must create and consolidate the conditions for the existence, survival, growth and expansion of our army among the people …

'In preparation to root our political and military units among the people we must take cognisance of the fact that we need to develop our work … in the urban and rural areas. We have to rally substantial numbers of the oppressed and exploited working class, the discarded, harassed and landless peasantry and persecuted and muzzled students and the intelligentsia. In the tackling of these countless tasks, let us regularly remind ourselves of what Lenin said: "Let us remember that a great mass struggle is approaching. The masses must know that they are entering upon an armed, bloody and desperate struggle. Contempt for death must become widespread among them and will ensure victory."'

Hani's quotation from Lenin was apt, if not prophetic. In the following year, after the establishment of the

United Democratic Front (UDF) in 1983, and the setback of the Nkomati Accord in March 1984, there was a series of mass uprisings, beginning in the Vaal Triangle towns in September, and spreading to the East Rand and other areas. People in the townships began to rise up in unarmed resistance against the imposition of new town councils and rent increases, and in protest about educational issues. When Oliver Tambo, in his ANC anniversary speech in January 1985, called upon the people of South Africa to make the country 'ungovernable', he was responding to a crisis that had already begun.

The ability of the ANC and of MK to respond to the popular demand for arms and military assistance was always limited by the lack, in spite of the earlier efforts of Hani and others, of an established underground. There was always a sense that the ANC and MK were not initiating mass actions, but reacting to, and sometimes failing to react to, the evolving situation on the ground. As late as 1991 Hani commented on the inability of MK to respond adequately to the popular demand for help in the setting up of self-defence units, which had been initiated in December 1990.

Chris Hani was a participant in the long-promised national consultative conference, which was held at Kabwe in Zambia in June 1985. In the elections for the NEC on that occasion, the first democratic elections in exile, he came top of the poll – an indication that his popularity had survived the crisis in Angola in the previous year – one of his most difficult moments – and that he retained the support of MK members. The decisions taken at the conference included the opening of positions in the NEC to non-African members, but for many of the participants, including Thabo Mbeki and Joel Netshitenzhe, the most important decision related to the intensification of 'people's war'.

The mood of the conference was influenced by the South African special forces' attack on Gaborone, in which 14 ANC members were killed, two days before it opened. There was a demand for the intensification of armed struggle and a move away from sabotage towards attacks on the personnel running the apartheid system. This view had been pithily expressed in a story about stick-fighting told in isiXhosa by the Thembu paramount, King Sabata Dalindyebo, who had been in exile in Lusaka since 1980. The wife of a man who appears to be losing shouts: 'What's the matter, my husband? You are much stronger than him and a better fighter, but he's defeating you. You are losing because you have only one stick in one hand, while your other hand is useless because it is stupidly holding a blanket to cover your nakedness. Drop the blanket, forget your nakedness, and fight with both hands!' The conference was enthusiastic about 'people's war', but rejected any suggestion of 'terrorism'. At the press conference afterwards, Oliver Tambo said that the distinction between 'soft' and 'hard' targets would disappear in 'an intensified confrontation ... an escalating conflict'.

At the same time Tambo told the conference that the ANC would not enter into talks with the South African government, but would be meeting with a group of 'important people' from South Africa. This was a reference to the delegation led by Gavin Relly, chairman of Anglo American Corporation, which met with an ANC delegation at President Kaunda's lodge at Mfuwe in the Luangwa National Park in September 1985. The delegation included Tony Bloom of Premier Milling and several journalists from English- and Afrikaans-language newspapers in South Africa. The ANC team included Oliver Tambo, Thabo Mbeki, Mac Maharaj, Pallo Jordan, James Stuart and Hani, who was clearly there to represent MK. He was the only member of the ANC delegation who was not wearing a business suit and was, like the visiting businessmen, informally dressed. According to the detailed notes of the meeting kept by Tony Bloom, he made only one intervention. He insisted that while the ANC was accused of violence, it was President P.W. Botha who was the violent one, using the instruments and institutions of the state. The people in the townships, where a state of emergency had recently been declared, were faced by tanks, guns and police. He did not think that Botha was sincere in his talk of reform.

A gap was soon to emerge between Hani and Thabo Mbeki over the question of negotiations, but it was not obvious at this stage. Mbeki made two interventions in which he stressed the need for the intensification of military as well as political struggle. He insisted, however, that the ANC had not changed its position at the Kabwe Conference on the avoidance of civilian casualties and that the members of the ANC were the real moderates. Hani did not play a major role in the series of meetings with deputations from inside South Africa that followed the Mfuwe meeting. He was not present at the meeting in Dakar with Afrikaner intellectuals in 1987, but he was one of the leaders who met Desmond Tutu, then Bishop of Johannesburg, on his first visit to Lusaka in March of that year.

He was, however, furious that neither he, nor other members of the NEC, were consulted or informed about the talks that Mbeki initiated, with Tambo's consent, in February 1988 with a group of Afrikaner intellectuals led by Professor Willie Esterhuyse of Stellenbosch University, who was acting as a conduit to South African intelligence, at Mells Park in England. At a meeting of the National Working Committee that was chaired by Alfred Nzo, the secretary-general, in the absence of Tambo, he asked: 'On whose authority has Cde Thabo entered into negotiations with these Afrikaner intellectuals?' Receiving the support of the other members of the committee, Hani demanded: 'Let the minutes record that we register our extreme displeasure that Cde Thabo has unilaterally gone to London without any … consultation and without a mandate from the NEC.'

Although the press later played up the rivalry between Hani and Mbeki, they travelled together to the Soviet Union with their wives for a holiday in July 1988. Vladimir Shubin, one of their hosts, recalled that he asked both Mbeki and Hani separately: 'When do you think you will win?' Hani thought that the struggle would take another ten years. Mbeki accurately predicted that they would be home in 1990. This difference of opinion reflected their contrasting diplomatic and military perspectives.

In an interview with John Battersby in 1988, Hani said that it would not take five years, but many years, to persuade South Africa's whites that apartheid was too expensive in terms of their personal security to maintain. 'We must make apartheid expensive and costly in terms of lives. It must be made painful. At the moment it is very sweet for them, but it must be made painful and bitter, especially for the whites. It is bitter for the blacks. For the whites it must be made very painful and bitter.' In the same interview he had made clear the difference between his approach and that of Mbeki. He indicated that not only black South Africans, but even some white South Africans, were coming round to the view that 'apartheid won't just be destroyed through talking, but, since it is a violent system, it will be destroyed by revolutionary violence'.

Hani had played a leading role in the intensification of MK activities, including the targeted assassination of collaborators with the regime, black police officers and participants in community councils, and, from Botswana in December 1985, in the planting of landmines in border areas. These were aimed at white farmers, who were seen as co-opted members of the South African security apparatus. Between 1984 and 1988 there was a dramatic increase in the number of incidents that could be attributed to MK or to township militants acting on their own – these increased from 45 in 1984 to 137 in 1985, 230 in 1986, and 235 in 1987. They peaked at 282 in 1988. By 1986 incidents were occurring all over the country and not just in the Transvaal and Natal, as had previously been the case. There were, however, problems with this intensification and the move towards 'soft' targets.

In 1985–86 there was a spate of attacks on Wimpy Bars in which civilians were killed. This culminated in the attack on Magoo's Bar in Durban in June 1986 when three people were killed and 69 injured. In the following year Tambo sent Mac Maharaj and Cassius Make to the frontline states to restrain MK units from actions that were seen as counterproductive. The strategy of laying landmines in border areas also proved to be a mistake, as there were many casualties among farm labourers and tractor-drivers – not the intended targets. It was soon abandoned. In 1986 neither Tambo nor Hani was prepared to condemn outright the practice of 'necklacing' – the burning alive of suspected spies and collaborators. By 1988 the ANC had taken a position against this practice and they were both prepared to speak out against it.

In an interview at the end of 1986 Hani took some pride in the success of MK assassination squads in the 'elimination' of black collaborators with the regime. He referred to the assassination of Brigadier Molope in the Bophuthatswana Bantustan and of Piet Ntuli in KwaNdebele. He also referred to the overrunning of a police station in the Transkei during which ten policemen were killed. The assassinations of Molope, and of a notorious security policeman in Mamelodi (a Pretoria township), as well as of David Lukhele, a promoter of the failed Land Deal between South Africa and Swaziland, were carried out by a group, later known as the Delmas Four, which reported directly to Hani. It is not, however, certain that he approved of all their targets.

These assassinations were a response to the murders of ANC leaders in the frontline states, which had begun with the killing by parcel bomb of John Dube in Lusaka in 1974, and had continued through the murder, among many others, of Joe Gqabi in Harare in 1981, and of Ruth First in Maputo in the following year, as well as the raids on ANC houses in Maputo in 1981, in Maseru in 1982 and 1985, and in Gaborone in the latter year. They were also a response to the activities of hit squads, run from Vlakplaas, near Pretoria, by policemen such as Dirk Coetzee and Eugene de Kock, which had taken many lives, including those of Griffiths and Victoria Mxenge. Although the killing of uniformed combatants was seen as legitimate, the Truth and Reconciliation Commission later condemned the extra-judicial killing of town councillors, askaris and people who had given evidence against the ANC as state witnesses, as gross violations of human rights.

Hani was also proud of the role played by MK in support of mass action in urban areas, in Cape Town, Johannesburg, Pretoria and Durban. 'We introduced an armed element to the mass struggles of our people in KTC, Crossroads, Alexandra, Mamelodi, in White City Jabavu, and in Rockville, and we are even beginning to defend our people against the rampaging brutal activities of Inkatha ka Zulu in Umlazi, in Clermont and KwaMashu. We have become part and parcel of the ongoing mass struggles of our people. As far as I am concerned, we are very optimistic that MK continues to grow and strengthen its capacity to confront the enemy.'

At an uncertain date in 1986 or 1987 Hani also played a significant part in the establishment of Operation Vula, a scheme to place a member of the NEC, Mac Maharaj, underground in South Africa to liaise with members of the Mass Democratic Movement (MDM). This was Maharaj's brainchild, but he recruited Hani to put the proposal to the NEC. The proposal was seconded by Jacob Zuma and passed without debate. The project was then managed in great secrecy by Tambo and Joe Slovo. Maharaj finally entered South Africa with Siphiwe Nyanda, an MK commander, through Swaziland in August 1988. Hani was one of the few members of the NEC who were aware of Vula and he was also one of the few who defended it when it was exposed in July 1990. Maharaj's activities were confined to the Transvaal and Natal, and it was expected that Hani would himself enter South Africa to operate in the Western Cape – preparations were made for this, but he did not enter the country. It is not entirely clear why not, but in 1987 he succeeded Joe Slovo as chief of staff of MK and this may have made him indispensable in Lusaka. Slovo gave up his MK role in order to become general secretary of the SACP.

MK activity stalled after 1988 as a result of the military occupation of many of South Africa's townships, the pressures exerted on Swaziland, Botswana, Lesotho and Mozambique to deny it rear bases, and the enforced withdrawal from Angola after the agreement concluded at the end of the year between South Africa and Angola. This was in exchange for the withdrawal of Cuban forces and paved the way for Namibian independence. Hani was involved as commissar in organising MK's move from Angola to Uganda, where its new camps were far from the front line and conditions were initially poor. There was at the same time strong pressure on MK from the NEC to increase military activity in South Africa as a way of increasing the political pressure on the regime and disrupting the municipal council elections that were planned for October 1988. Pushing young men, and a few women, across the border to fend for themselves, with a still inadequately developed underground, resulted in heavy casualties, and many people, facing the prospect of death, were turned by the regime and became askaris.

The resignation of P.W. Botha from the South African presidency and the succession of F.W. de Klerk in August 1989, and the release of Walter Sisulu and all the other Rivionia Trial prisoners, with the single exception of Nelson Mandela, in September, indicated a quickening of the pace of change towards negotiations. But speaking to a journalist in Lusaka soon after the visit of Sisulu and others to Lusaka in January 1990, and ten days before the unbanning of the ANC, Hani continued to take a hard line on armed struggle and a sceptical view of negotiations. In an implied criticism of Mbeki he said: 'Now we want to take this question of negotiations away from the clever initiatives and manoeuvres of individuals. We want to put it squarely in the hands of the people. The people must know that negotiations is [sic] an arena of struggle. They must know that negotiations are not going to be possible through offers from the ruling class.'

When asked if De Klerk could not seize the initiative by unbanning the ANC and releasing political prisoners, he said: 'I believe the armed struggle will continue if the ANC is unbanned. Because the regime will still use violence ... will still resort to its military and security forces ... Do you think overnight now the regime will stop beating up the workers, shooting workers, dispersing demonstrators[?] Will it stop raiding homes? Will it stop using its security laws to ban people and to detain people[?]'

It would be necessary, he said, to go on building MK even during a temporary ceasefire and 'to teach our cadres that there is a need to fight and talk and if talks fail we must go back and fight'. Drawing on the example of Algeria, he compared De Klerk to General Charles de Gaulle, who had been a prisoner of the right wing, but had eventually broken with it. He thought that De Klerk needed the ANC's help to break out. He asked whether De Klerk might not be replaced by someone further to the right such as Andries Treurnicht 'who would bring about bloodshed for another ten years, or whether [the whites] would like a leader who would negotiate for a democratic solution to our problems'.

Hani was in Lusaka attending a meeting of the Politico-Military Council on 2 February 1990 when the meeting was interrupted by the announcement of the unbanning of the ANC and the release of Mandela. Hani was the first to respond: 'Nothing has changed. We need to infiltrate *more* cadres and arms into the country!'

At an MK seminar in April 1990 Joe Modise, while conceding that MK actions had peaked in 1988, and that it had never been able to establish itself in rural areas or construct a 'Ho Chi Minh trail', called for further measures to destabilise the regime. At the same time he envisaged the transformation of MK into a well-trained, regular and modern army. At a meeting in Lusaka in May, which had been organised by IDASA (Institute for a Democratic Alternative in South Africa), leaders of MK, including Hani, met with 46 people from South Africa, including retired Defence Force officers, and serving officers in Bantustan armies, as well as conscripts and members of the End Conscription Campaign. Hani may have moderated his views a little after the release of Mandela, but he still rejected calls for 'our unilateral abandonment of the armed struggle in the face of persistent political and armed brutality ... [and] a battery of laws preventing free political activity whilst giving sweeping powers to the South African security establishment'.

Hani was expected to return to South Africa with an advance party including Jacob Zuma in March, but he did not do so. He returned with the main group of the leadership, including Thabo Mbeki and Joe Slovo, on 28 April. He was back in Lusaka in May for the IDASA meeting and for one with a Cuban delegation, where further military training was discussed, and seems to have delayed his return to South Africa until June. In the following month Operation Vula became public knowledge after the arrest of Siphiwe Nyanda, Mac Maharaj and others. Hani was one of the few leaders of the ANC who spoke in support of Vula. It may not have been cause and effect, but his indemnity against prosecution was withdrawn and he moved to the Transkei, where its military ruler, Brigadier Bantu Holomisa, granted him political asylum.

Responding to strong international pressure and a proposal from Joe Slovo, the ANC decided on 22 July 1990 to declare a ceasefire, but it did not announce this until 6 August. Hani was shocked when he heard the news through a broadcast press conference and said in a later interview: 'I didn't want it. I was annoyed. I was marooned in the Transkei when the decision was taken to suspend armed struggle ... without comprehensive consultation.' He had, he said, spent 27 years in MK – the better part of his life – and when he heard the announcement he felt like crying. But when it was explained to him that the ceasefire was necessary to maintain the momentum of negotiations, he accepted it and justified it to others.

Hani was not much involved in the transitional negotiations, but he did attend the meeting in Durban in February 1991 that produced the D.F. Malan Accord – a refinement of the earlier Pretoria Minute. The ANC undertook to stop the infiltration of arms and personnel and not to create new underground structures or recruit for training inside South Africa. It did not, however, agree to surrender its arms caches or stop setting up self-defence units. The government agreed to accelerate the granting of indemnities and the release of political prisoners. The ANC continued to import arms until 1993, justifying its breach of this agreement with reference to the government's sponsorship of 'third force' activities. It was not until after democratic elections in April 1994 that the ANC handed over its arms during the integration of

MK into the new South African National Defence Force.

At the first ANC National Conference since its unbanning in July 1991, Hani once again came top of the poll in the elections for the NEC with 95 per cent of the possible votes – Thabo Mbeki came a close second. In the later election by members of the newly elected NEC for the National Working Committee, the places were reversed and Hani came second to Mbeki. Hani had apparently forced Mbeki to drop out of the race for the deputy presidency at the same conference by saying that he would run against him if he stood. His determination to stop Mbeki may have been the result of a long-standing rivalry, but also the result of a clash between Slovo and Hani, on the one hand, and Mbeki, Zuma, and several other members of the central committee, on the other hand, in connection with the re-launch of the SACP in July 1990. Slovo and Hani thought that all members of the central committee should 'come out' publicly as members at the re-launch, but Mbeki and Zuma disagreed and left the central committee and the party. As many as half the members of the central committee stepped down at this time.

In August 1991 Hani supported a move by Joe Slovo and Cyril Ramaphosa, the newly elected secretary-general of the ANC, without reference to Nelson Mandela, to remove Mbeki and Zuma from their roles as leader and deputy leader of the team that was negotiating with the government. They were unhappy with the slow pace of progress in negotiations, the granting of indemnities and the release of political prisoners. There may also have been a feeling that Ramaphosa had more experience as a negotiator than Mbeki, who was thought by some to be both too accommodating and too secretive.

Hani spent a good deal of time in the Transkei in 1990–91 and stayed for a while in the ministerial housing complex in Umtata, but he also travelled internationally. He accompanied Mandela to the United States in 1990 and was there again in April 1991 on a fundraising tour for the SACP. He addressed a dinner in San Francisco attended by 800 people and chaired by Angela Davis, the American communist and feminist.

According to some accounts, he was involved in the planning of MK actions from the Transkei – if so, they were in breach of the ceasefire, and this seems unlikely. Members of MK helped Holomisa to suppress an attempted coup in November 1990, which was orchestrated through elements of the Transkei Defence Force by South African military intelligence. Hani took refuge in the Transkei for a second time following the withdrawal of his indemnity in July 1991. He was, however, able to be present at the MK conference at the University of Venda in the following month.

In his speech on that occasion he referred to the difficulties that MK had experienced in Uganda, Tanzania and Zambia. He acknowledged that the camps had been neglected following the return of members of MHQ to

South Africa and their preoccupation with the internal situation. It was necessary, he said, to deal with the consequences of the ceasefire. 'An idle army is the devil's workshop and we are likely to face battalions of problems if we do not solve the problems of deployment.' The MK underground would have to remain in place until 'we have reached a point of irreversibility in the negotiation process'. He also indicated that progress had been made in the previous three years in the training of regular army officers in the Soviet Union, but its disintegration, which was reaching a climax as he spoke, made this difficult and there was a need to find alternative places for training.

He outlined his vision of a new democratic South Africa and of the army's role in it. 'As we build a new democratic society, we have to hammer out a new value system that must reinforce the freedom of the individual and competitive politics. But we must realise that years of national repression has [*sic*] made the present society complex and divided. These complexities and divisions are even more acute during this period of transition. The priority during this transition period and onwards is to reconcile all South Africans by creating understanding of a common and shared future within a new and just constitutional dispensation.'

He pointed out that the military operated 'in the midst of different political interests and social conflicts' and it was necessary to maintain high standards of professionalism, impartiality and tolerance. 'Members of the security forces must be oriented towards participation in a democratic society both as citizens and soldiers with a full knowledge of the values they must protect.' MK had developed in a political tradition where the bottom line was the seizure of power, but that was no longer on the agenda. Barring a major disaster in the negotiations process, the transition was likely to be 'relatively peaceful' and a new army would be composed from MK, the South African Defence Force and the various Bantustan armies. They should, however, not allow a situation 'where the dominant and central positions are solely in the hands of those that have fought and struggled against democracy'.

This important speech was his swansong as a military leader and was typical in its emphasis on the political. He was already making plans to step down as MK chief of staff and to take over from Joe Slovo as general secretary of the SACP. When Nelson Mandela announced this possibility to the conference, there was a strongly adverse reaction and a popular demand that Hani should stay with MK. At the SACP conference in December, he was, however, elected general secretary and stepped down as chief of staff. In the same month he participated in the Convention for a Democratic South Africa (CODESA), the first formal negotiations, as the leading spokesperson for the SACP.

In his speech on that occasion he demanded the release of all political prisoners and the return of exiles, the formation of an Interim Government of National Unity, and elections for a constituent assembly. He supported a multi-party democracy, but said that political freedom without social reconstruction would be meaningless. There was a need for a new growth path which would create wealth more efficiently than the present economic policies. He also pointed to the examples of Angola and Mozambique and warned of the danger of civil war.

It is sometimes said that Hani, Slovo and other 'hardliners' in the SACP lacked commitment to negotiations and continued to hope for a revolutionary seizure of power. There is no evidence to support this view and plenty of evidence to refute it. According to Vladimir Shubin, a well-informed source, both Slovo and Hani were convinced as early as 1986 that there would be a negotiated settlement. Hani told Shubin in November 1986 that the next government of South Africa – he did not indicate when it would be formed – would be a government of national unity, composed of representatives of the ANC, the National Party and other groups. The subject of future talks between the ANC and the government would be the calling of a Constitutional Assembly.

Hani and Slovo were, however, less trusting of their apartheid interlocutors than, for example, Thabo Mbeki, and thought that continued mass action was necessary to put pressure on the government to bring negotiations to a favourable conclusion. After a deadlock was reached in the CODESA talks in May 1992, the ANC launched a programme of rolling mass action and broke off contact with the government after the Boipatong massacre in June.

As part of this campaign of action, Hani, together with Steve Tshwete, Ronnie Kasrils and other ANC leaders, participated in the march on Bisho, the capital of the Ciskei Bantustan, in September. The ANC had demanded the right to campaign throughout the country and the removal of the Ciskei ruler, Brigadier Gqozo, who refused to allow it to operate in his area. When the government declined to act, the ANC decided on a peaceful march from King William's Town to Bisho. Twenty-eight marchers were killed when units of the Ciskeian Defence Force opened fire on the unarmed marchers. Hani and the other leaders were fortunate to escape with their lives. Ronnie Kasrils recalls that Hani displayed great physical courage and was tireless in rallying the crowds after this tragic event. He had no doubt that the attack on the crowd at Bisho had been orchestrated from Pretoria which was pursuing a twin-track policy of negotiations together with 'the systematic deployment of violence as a central component of a political strategy'. The South African government was, in Hani's view, seeking to destabilise the ANC through the promotion of a low-intensity civil war, using surrogates such as Inkatha and the Bantustan defence forces.

Mandela and De Klerk met after this incident and some progress was made in bilateral talks between the

ANC and the National Party. The outlines of a settlement were put forward by Joe Slovo in a paper entitled 'Negotiations: What room for compromise?' By February 1993 there was agreement in principle on elections for a constituent assembly, on a five-year government of national unity in which all parties would be represented, and on 'sunset clauses', including guarantees for civil servants in the transitional period.

Hani addressing an ANC rally in Cape Town, 1993.
(Photo: Rashid Lombard)

9

Visions of a new South Africa

By the time Chris Hani became general secretary of the
SACP in December 1991, the Soviet Union had more
or less ceased to exist after the coup in August that
precipitated Gorbachev's resignation. During his long
military career Hani had held office within the SACP,
but he had not made many statements on its behalf. He
was always seen as close, both militarily and politically,
to Joe Slovo. They had welcomed Gorbachev and the
moves towards glasnost and perestroika. They had gone
with Tambo to the Soviet Union on the occasion of
his only meeting with Gorbachev in November 1986,
but they were not present at it. Only Thabo Mbeki
accompanied Tambo to the meeting, which lasted for
most of two hours.

They were clearly shocked by the collapse of
communism in Eastern Europe and the evidence for its
unpopularity in the Soviet Union. Hani was in agreement
with the thrust of Slovo's pamphlet *Has Socialism Failed?*
– published in January 1990 – that the Soviet model was

a distortion and had failed, but this did not discredit the ideals of socialism as such. In an interview shortly before his death, Hani conceded that they might have been blind, naïve or myopic in failing to see totalitarianism and a lack of democracy within the Soviet Union, but bad things done in the name of socialism did not discredit its basic principles any more than the principles of Christianity were damaged by bad things done in its name. He did not believe that the crisis in socialism was the end of history.

There was room, he said, for 'born-again socialists and communists', committed to pluralism and a multi-party system. They did not wish to impose socialism and would dispense with concepts such as 'the dictatorship of the proletariat'. At the SACP conference in December 1991 Hani and Slovo had both pressed for the adoption of the phrase 'democratic socialism' as a description of South African communism. Their proposal was rejected by the majority of delegates who felt that socialism was intrinsically democratic and there was no need to spell this out. The tendency of all Hani's later political pronouncements was, perhaps for pragmatic rather than ideological reasons, in the direction of social democracy and he sometimes referred to the Swedish model. He was insistent on the importance of building an open society, a civil society with strong civic associations, trade unions and churches. It was necessary to ensure that there were regular elections and that no government had unlimited power.

Hani acknowledged that as a leader of the SACP he was in the unusual position of heading a communist party that was growing rapidly at a time when many other communist parties were in decline. Membership of the SACP grew from less than 1,000 at the beginning of 1990 to as many as 25,000 by the end of 1991. There were people who thought he was making a mistake by stepping down from leadership positions within MK and the ANC in order to lead the SACP at a time when many leaders of the ANC had quietly abandoned it. Although Hani resigned from his position on the National Working Committee of the ANC, he retained his place on the NEC.

He made it clear that he intended to work with the ANC and COSATU for the achievement of the 'national democratic revolution'. The role of the SACP would now be different. It would no longer consist of a few members working within the ANC and COSATU – they would be building a strong and independent party to represent the interests of the workers and the poor. There was room for class struggle within the ANC.

Many people wonder today whether the removal of Chris Hani from the political scene made a significant difference to the later history of South Africa. If he had lived, how would he have influenced the political trajectory of the ANC and SACP? Would he have successfully opposed policies, such as Black Economic Empowerment (BEE), which have resulted in the enrichment of a small number of people but done little for the masses? Would he have led the

SACP, as Wolfie Kodesh wondered in 1993, into opposition to the ANC? Or would he, as his assassins apparently believed, have been Mandela's successor as leader of the ANC and president of South Africa?

The answer to such counter-factual questions is, of course, that we don't know and we can't know. It seems highly improbable that Mandela and the ANC would have allowed Hani, one of its most popular leaders, to remain outside government in 1994, as he apparently intended to do. Once in government, he would have been involved in controversial decisions like the abandonment of the Reconstruction and Development Programme (RDP) and the adoption of GEAR (Growth, Employment and Redistribution). The Anglo American Corporation's resident director in Zambia, Vernon Webber, had discussions with Hani in 1989–90 and thought that he was moving, like other members of the ANC and SACP, towards acceptance of the role of capital. Speaking to 200 businessmen at a meeting organised by *Finance Week* in September 1992, shortly after the Bisho massacre, he certainly sounded conciliatory. He accepted the need for economic growth and foreign investment, though with some redistribution. He did not reject the market, but said that the real problem was that 'the great majority of South Africa's people are not even *in* the market.' They were 'utterly marginalised, without resources and skills to sell'. Speaking about nationalisation, he made it clear on various occasions that he had not abandoned the idea, but that he was opposed to statist and bureaucratic models. He was interested in newer forms of worker control and participation in private industry.

Hani took progressive stands on many issues. He was well known for his feminism and acknowledged that sexism was embedded in the whole of South African society. It was, he said, a problem in MK and they had not succeeded in overcoming it. He was more conscious of, and outspoken about, the danger of HIV/AIDS than any other leader of the ANC and he said in 1990: 'We cannot allow the AIDS epidemic to ruin the realisation of our dreams.' Speaking to businessmen in 1992 he spoke of South Africa as an intensely violent society, pointing to Cape Town as the murder capital of the world and the country's rape statistics as the worst in the world. He had then pointed to the country's deep underlying problems: 'homelessness, joblessness, illiteracy, the lack of running water, the lack of electrification.'

Talking to Charles Villa-Vicencio in January 1993, Hani expressed concern for the returned exiles and soldiers who had expected to come home as conquerors, but who were standing in unemployment lines. 'We have limited time on our hands to redress this situation and must ensure that a democratic South Africa does not forget, or marginalise, those men and women who sacrificed everything in order to fight against apartheid and bring about democracy.

'Many are without education and without the kind of

skills necessary to earn a living. Unless we face up to the fact that we are in a post-war period of reconstruction, in which we are obliged to provide facilities and incentives to demobilised soldiers, we are in trouble.

'An increasing number of people will become quite cynical about government and society as a whole. This will be an explosive situation, likely to lead to open rebellion.

'The present [National Party] government is unlikely to do anything about this. They see this discontent as working in their favour, as an option for destabilising the ANC ...'

In conversation with his friend Tokyo Sexwale, shortly before his death, he expressed concern about the unemployed youth and spoke of a people's Peace Corps to replace the self-defence units. 'Somehow we have to solve the problems faced by the black youth in South Africa. They are poor. They are uneducated because they have had access only to the terrible Bantu Education system. This makes them restless and hungry for revenge ... The youth should be trained to defend their community which is one of the aims of a Peace Corps ... one day the youth will be ruling this country and they must be properly prepared for that day. The Peace Corps should be used to train them for this.'

He took a strong line on rural feudalism and the institution of chieftainship. It was not democratic and the chiefs had over the years been collaborating

124

in the oppression of the rural poor. There was a need to democratise the rural areas. The ANC recognised chieftainship, but it could not be allowed to exist in the old way. 'We cannot accept a situation where the chiefs have got vetoing powers over the democratic decision of the majority of the people.' Chiefs should no longer be able to impose their views on poor people.

He was wary of the growth of the security apparatus. 'I am allergic to a powerful security force which is unaccountable. In a small way I have seen it in the ANC where the security will whisper to the leaders, "You know so and so is not to be trusted."' He believed strongly in freedom of expression and that 'free citizens make for a stronger state'.

In a later tribute Pallo Jordan, a non-communist member of the ANC's leadership, and a critic of the SACP, wrote: 'Comrade Chris Hani was among those South African Communists prepared to accept that the party had not always had an adequate appreciation of the dialectics of race, class and gender. He was consequently always open to discourse on these matters and did not arrogantly dismiss the views of non-party Marxists. His long stay in independent Africa had forced him to contend with the reality that independence had in many respects failed the ordinary people who had struggled for it. The emergence of rapacious indigenous elites – the wa-Benzis – with their life-style of conspicuous consumption disgusted him more than the colonial arrogance of the settler bourgeoisie. While he understood well the difficulties African states encountered in devising sustainable development programmes, he refused to offer alibis for the abuses and crimes ostensibly committed in defence of hard-won independence. Within the ANC alliance too he would not keep silent about the abuse of power and incipient corrupt practices. There were occasions on which he personally suffered for holding such views.'

* * *

Chris Hani had survived many assassination attempts in Lesotho and on his return to South Africa. He appears, however, to have had a premonition of his early death and gave a number of interviews within days of his assassination in which he enunciated his vision for the new South Africa. The most remarkable of these interviews was with an old friend, the radical journalist and SACP member, Wolfie Kodesh, with whom he had been in exile in Zambia.

Speaking to Kodesh on 1 April 1993, he said: 'I am an implacable enemy of oppression. I am a soldier for democracy and justice. Negotiations are a product of all our sacrifices – those who went to jail, those into exile, those in camps in strange countries. What is happening is the fruit of this hard worthwhile labour ... We need to build strong grass roots structures. We must build a popular democracy. A grassroots democracy.'

When Kodesh, bearing in mind Hani's recent statement that he did not intend to seek office in a government of national unity, asked him whether he envisaged the SACP as a kind of opposition to the government, as a watchdog for those whose expectations were not being realised, he replied that the SACP should remain within the ANC: 'NO, Wolfie, we must be everywhere. We must be in parliament. [In m]ass organisation. We must mobilise for reconstruction ... The ANC should not easily surrender to new forces who have a new agenda of elitism and bureaucracy and obliviousness of the majority of population. The alliance is determined by the objective situation. But as good communists we must analyze at each stage and adjust tactics and strategy. We need to stop violence. The political violence we can handle. The socio-economic violence is difficult. The regime has never bothered to remove the socio-economic causes of violence: the hostels; the deterioration in schools; the poverty and so on.'

Elsewhere, explaining his decision to stay out of government, he said: 'The perks of a new government are not really appealing to me. Everybody, of course, would like to have a good job, a good salary, and that sort of thing. But for me, that is not the be-all of a struggle. What is important is the continuation of the struggle – and we must accept that the struggle is always continuing – under different conditions whether within parliament or outside parliament, we shall begin to tackle the real problems of the country. And the real problems of the country are not whether one is in cabinet, or a key minister, but what we do for social upliftment of the working masses of our people.'

And, prophetically, he said: 'I think finally the ANC will have to fight a new enemy. That enemy would be another struggle to make freedom and democracy worthwhile to ordinary South Africans. Our biggest enemy would be what we do in the field of socio-economic restructuring: creation of jobs; building houses, schools, medical facilities; overhauling our education; eliminating illiteracy, building a society which cares, and fighting corruption and ... the gravy train of using power, government position to enrich individuals. We must build a different culture in this country, different from Africa, different from the Nationalist Party. And that culture should be one of service to people.'

Hani had a religious cast of mind, whether as Catholic or communist. He said that he was an atheist, but his widow, Limpho, said that he asked her and his three daughters to pray for him at times of crisis, and she believed that he died a Christian. He was given a Catholic funeral, but he was not a saint. He could, like most people, be vain, moody and petulant, though he was mainly noted for his jovial good humour and his ability to light up a room. Some critics accused him of ethnic chauvinism, of gathering a clique of Xhosa-speaking people around him, but almost everyone acknowledged that he was a man of courage and compassion.

He had displayed his physical courage again and again: during the Wankie Campaign; in the campaigns against UNITA, and in confronting MK mutineers, in Angola; in entering apartheid South Africa as an underground operative; and in risking assassination in Lesotho, on visits to other forward areas, and on his return home to South Africa. A fitness fanatic, he had never allowed considerations of security to stop him jogging around Lusaka or Boksburg.

He had also shown outstanding moral courage, and may have risked his life, in becoming the primary writer and lead signatory of the Hani Memorandum, the most outspoken internal critique of the ANC in exile. He continued to show moral courage in his campaigns within the ANC against executions, torture and the appalling conditions at Quatro, and in his demand for a commission of inquiry into the death of Thami Zulu. Some people thought that he displayed courage in assuming the leadership of the SACP at a time when other leaders were abandoning it, and in declaring his intention to stay out of government.

It was almost certainly the quality of compassion, his ability to listen to rank-and-file members of the ANC, as well as his impressive physical presence, that made him such an attractive person. The Reverend Michael Lapsley, who worked closely with him in Lesotho, said of him in a film interview: 'That compassion for comrades was quite wonderful – a great virtue – because the toughness of the struggle hardened some people. The commitment to power hardened some people. The fact that he retained that tenderness and concern for others who didn't have voices because of their position was a great virtue and one of the reasons why people loved him so much.'

Mandla Langa, poet and novelist, and a leading member of the ANC's Arts and Culture Department in exile, recalled: 'Young and old, trainees or veterans, all gravitated towards Hani, for he had that unique talent of animating discussions to solve problems. Whether in Lesotho or Lusaka, there would always be a group around him, drawn to something that resonated with their own understanding of the world and of themselves. These discussions, mainly political, were conducted in a language everyone could understand. Hani loved simplicity ... To remember Hani is to evoke the memory of all that was great about our people in struggle. It is to remember the hardship and the sacrifice, the joy and exultation of people with a vision. It is to recall the setbacks, skirmishes and losses – and the need, even then, to march on, knowing that the enemy had no moral standing.'

Hani clearly combined an exceptional ability to listen with extraordinary eloquence, which shines through his extempore interviews. Bill Anderson, who worked in MK's military intelligence, says that 'Chris was a wonderful commissar who would care for every cadre who asked him for support'. There are accounts of queues of people waiting to see him to discuss personal problems, whether in the Angolan camps or in Lusaka. While Mandla Langa points to his ability to animate discussion to solve problems, Howard Barrell compares him with Steve Biko for his ability to inspire people to positive action.

Joe Slovo, the man to whom Hani was closest in the ANC and SACP, and who survived him by less than two years, paid him this moving tribute in a filmed interview after his death: 'Unlike a few other communists who then saw the fleshpots of power looming, with the ANC being the vehicle, Chris did not allow that to influence his commitment and I think perhaps the greatest thing one can say about him is that, being aware that he must give up his position as chief of staff of MK, and ... as a member of the Working Committee of the ANC ... he nevertheless chose ... to take the path of commitment rather than ambition.'

Hani showed more awareness than most leaders of the danger that the ANC would be corrupted by power and seduced by the temptations of office. He had clearly read the works of Frantz Fanon, probably in Lusaka in the late 1960s with his friend Ben Magubane, and he was fully aware from his own experience of the danger that people in office would forget the urban and rural poor – that nationalist movements tended to be captured by the emergent middle classes who used power in their own interests and for their own enrichment. He never forgot his own rural roots and spent time at Sabalele within weeks of his death. From the time of the Wankie Campaign and the Hani Memorandum, he had been consistently outspoken in his criticism of what he thought was wrong with the ANC in exile, and he was never doctrinaire in his commitment to Marxism-Leninism. He insisted that tolerance of internal criticism, as displayed in exile by Oliver Tambo, was something that the ANC must carry with it into the future.

Postscript

Chris Hani was assassinated by Janusz Waluś with a gun supplied by Clive Derby-Lewis on Easter Saturday 10 April 1993. His funeral took place on 19 April at the FNB stadium, Soweto, and he was buried at Elspark Cemetery, Germiston, a site that he had chosen not long before his death. Waluś and Derby-Lewis were found guilty of his murder and sentenced to death in October 1993. Derby-Lewis's wife, Gaye, was acquitted of the same charge. Among the witnesses at the trial was Margarita Harmse, the woman whom Mandela mentioned in his broadcast on the day of the murder. The death penalty was declared unconstitutional in June 1995 and their appeals against sentence were rejected in November 1995. Their applications to the Truth and Reconciliation Commission for amnesty were rejected in April 1999 on the grounds that they had not shown that they were acting for a political organisation and had not fully disclosed the background to their crime. Derby-Lewis was released on medical parole in June 2015 and died in November 2016. Waluś was denied parole in March 2020 and remains in prison today.

A Black Sash vigil outside City Hall, Cape Town, April 1993.
(Photo: Rashid Lombard)

Acknowledgements

I am grateful to Professor William Beinart, the Leverhulme Trust and the African Studies Centre, Oxford University, for sponsoring, funding and hosting the research work in Zambia and South Africa on which this book, and my earlier book, *The Lusaka years: The ANC in exile in Zambia, 1963–94* (Jacana Media, 2013), are based. I would like to repeat my thanks to all the people who are mentioned in the acknowledgements and list of interviewees that appear in the earlier book. I would like in addition to thank Bill Anderson, Howard Barrell, Arianna Lissoni, May McClain, Mavuso Msimang and Lucy Graham for help with this book. I am also grateful to Greg Houston and James Ngculu for access to the unpublished long version of the biographical essay that prefaces their edited book *Voices of liberation: Chris Hani* (HSRC Press, 2014). Their book prints many of the documentary sources and interviews on which this book draws and is an invaluable resource.

Bibliography

Published books and articles

Amnesty International, *South Africa: Torture, executions and ill-treatment in African National Congress camps*, London, December 1992

Anonymous, 'Chris Hani: A drawing by a close political activist', *Dawn*, 25th anniversary of MK, [1986]

Barrell, Howard, *MK: The ANC's armed struggle*, London: Penguin Books, 1990

Berger, Michele, *They fought for freedom: Chris Hani*, Cape Town: Maskew Miller, Longman, 1994

Bernstein, Hilda, *The rift: The exile experience of South Africans*, London: Jonathan Cape, 1994

Binda, Alex (comp. and ed. by Chris Collins), *The Saints: The Rhodesian Light Infantry*, Johannesburg: Galago Books, 2007

Bopela, Thula, and Daluxolo Luthuli, *Umkhonto we Sizwe: Fighting for a divided people*, Alberton: Galago, 2005

Bottoman, W.W. *The making of an MK cadre*, Pretoria: LiNc Publishers, 2010

Braam, Conny, *Operation Vula*, Johannesburg: Jacana Media, 2004

Bundy, Colin, *Govan Mbeki*, Johannesburg: Jacana Media, 2012

Butler, Anthony, *Cyril Ramaphosa*, Johannesburg: Jacana Media, 2008

Callinicos, Luli, *Oliver Tambo: Beyond the Engeli mountains*, Cape Town: David Philip, 2004

Cherry, Janet, *Umkhonto weSizwe*, Johannesburg: Jacana Media, 2011

Cronin, Jeremy, review of Stephen Ellis and Tsepo Sechaba, *Comrades against apartheid*, in *Work in Progress*, 8, 1992

Derrida, Jacques, *Specters of Marx: The state of the debt, the work of mourning, and the new international*, London: Routledge, 1994

Dingake, Michael, *My fight against apartheid*, London: Kliptown Books, 1987

Douek, D., '"They became afraid when they saw us": MK insurgency and counterinsurgency in the Bantustan of Transkei, 1988–94', *Journal of Southern African Studies*, 39(1) 2013

Ellis, Stephen, and Tsepo Sechaba, *Comrades against apartheid: The ANC and SACP in exile*, London: James Currey, 1992

Ellis, Stephen, *External mission: The ANC in exile, 1960–1990*, Johannesburg: Jonathan Ball, 2012

Flower, Ken, *Serving secretly: An intelligence chief on record, Rhodesia into Zimbabwe, 1964–81*, London: John Murray, 1987

Gerhart, G.M., and C. Glaser (eds), *From protest to challenge*, vol. 6: *Challenge and victory, 1980–1990*, Bloomington: Indiana University Press, 2010

Gevisser, Mark, *Thabo Mbeki: The dream deferred*, Johannesburg: Jonathan Ball, 2007

Gibbs, Timothy, *Mandela's kinsmen: Nationalist elites and apartheid's first bantustan*, Johannesburg: Jacana Media, 2014

Hani, Chris, 'Hani opens up', interview with Hein Marais, *Work in Progress*, 82, May–June 1992

Hani, Chris, 'How possible is peace?', address to function organised by *Finance Week*, September 1992, *African Communist*, 3rd quarter, 1992

Hani, Chris, 'The Wankie campaign', in *Dawn, 25th anniversary of MK*, [1986]

Harris, Peter, *In a different time: The inside story of the Delmas Four*, Cape Town: Umuzi, 2008

Hassim, Shireen, 'Nationalism, feminism and autonomy: The ANC in exile and the question of women', *Journal of Southern African Studies*, 30(4) 2004

Jordan, Pallo (ed.), *Oliver Tambo remembered*, Johannesburg: Macmillan South Africa, 2007

Karis, T., and G. Carter (eds), *From protest to challenge*, vol. 4, *Political profiles*, Stanford: Hoover Institution Press, 1977

Karis, T., and G. Gerhart (eds.), *From Protest to Challenge*, vol. 5: *Nadir and resurgence*, Bloomington: Indiana University Press, 1997

Kasrils, Ronnie, *Armed and dangerous: My underground struggle against apartheid*, 3rd edn, Johannesburg: Jacana Media, 2013

Macmillan, Hugh, 'The Hani memorandum: introduced and annotated', *Transformation*, 69, 2009

Macmillan, Hugh, *The Lusaka years: The ANC in exile, 1963–94*, Johannesburg: Jacana Media, 2013

Macmillan, Hugh, 'The story of a house – 250 Zambezi Road, Roma Township, Lusaka: The Simons, the ANC and Oxfam', in Robin Palmer (ed.), *A house in Zambia: Recollections of the ANC and Oxfam at 250 Zambezi Road, Lusaka, 1967–97*, Lusaka: Bookworld Publishers, 2008

Magubane, Bernard (with Mbulelo Mzamane), *My life and times*, Scottsville: University of KwaZulu-Natal Press, 2010

Maharaj, Zarina, *Dancing to a different rhythm*, Cape Town: Zebra Press, 2006

Mali, T. (ed. I. Vladislavić), *Chris Hani: The sun that set before dawn*, Johannesburg: Sached, 2000

Maloka, Eddy, *The South African Communist Party: Exile and after apartheid*, Johannesburg: Jacana Media, 2013

Mandela, Nelson, *Long walk to freedom: The autobiography of Nelson Mandela*, Randburg: Macdonald Purnell, 1994

Mangcu, Xolela, *Biko: A biography*, Cape Town: Tafelberg, 2012

Manghezi, Nadja, *The Maputo connection: ANC life in the world of Frelimo*, Johannesburg: Jacana, 2007

Mbali, Fanele, *In Transit: Autobiography of a South African freedom-fighter*, Johannesburg: South African History Online, 2012

Mda, Zakes, *Sometimes there is a void: Memoirs of an outsider*, Johannesburg, Penguin, 2011

Ngcobo, Lauretta, *Prodigal daughters: Stories of South African women in exile*, Pietermaritzburg: University of KwaZulu-Natal Press, 2012

Ngculu, James, *The honour to serve: Recollections of an Umkhonto soldier*, Claremont: David Philip, 2009

Nkobi, Thomas, 'Crossing the Zambezi', *Dawn, 25th Anniversary of MK*, souvenir issue, [1986]

Nyangoni, C. and G. Nyandoro, *Zimbabwe independence movements: Select documents*, London: Rex Collings, 1979

O'Malley, Padraig, *Shades of difference: Mac Maharaj and the struggle for South Africa*, London: Viking, 2007

SADET, *The road to democracy in South Africa, 1960–70*, vol. 1, Cape Town: Zebra Press, 2004

SADET, *The road to democracy: South Africans telling their stories*, Johannesburg: SADET, 2008

Sampson, Anthony, *Mandela: The authorised biography*, Johannesburg: Jonathan Ball, 1999

Seekings, Jeremy, *The UDF: A history of the United Democratic Front in South Africa, 1983–91*, Cape Town: David Philip, 2000

Sellström, Tor (ed.), *National liberation in southern Africa: Regional and Swedish voices*, Uppsala: Nordiska Afrikainstitutet, 2002

Sellström, Tor, *Sweden and national liberation in southern Africa*, vols. 1 and 2, Uppsala: Nordiska Afrikainstitutet, 1999 and 2002

Shubin, Vladimir, *ANC: A view from Moscow*, Bellville: Mayibuye Books, 1999 and Johannesburg: Jacana Media, 2008

Sibeko, Archie (with Joyce Leeson), *Freedom in our lifetime*, Durban: Indicator Press, University of Natal, 1996

Simons, Ray Alexander, *All my life and all my strength*, Johannesburg: STE Publishers, 2004

Slovo, Joe, *Has socialism failed?*, Umsebenzi discussion pamphlet, Inkululeko Publications, n.p., [1990]

Slovo, Joe, 'J.B. Marks, communist, man of the people, fighter for freedom', *African Communist*, 95, 1983

Slovo, Joe, 'Negotiations: What room for compromise?', *African Communist*, 3rd quarter, 1992

Slovo, Joe, 'No middle road', in B. Davidson, Joe Slovo and Anthony R. Wilkinson, *Southern Africa: The new politics of revolution*, Harmondsworth: Penguin, 1976

Smith, Janet and Beauregard Tromp, *Hani: A life too short*, Johannesburg: Jonathan Ball, 2009

Sparg, M., J. Schreiner and G. Ansell (eds), *Comrade Jack: The political lectures and diary of Jack Simons*, Johannesburg: STE, 2001

Sparks, Allister, *Tomorrow is another country: The inside story of South Africa's negotiated revolution*, Sandton: Struik, 1994

Strachan, Garth, 'Indecent obsession', *Work in Progress*, September 1992

Suttner, Raymond, *The ANC Underground in South Africa*, Johannesburg: Jacana Media, 2008.

Trewhela, Paul, *Inside Quatro: Uncovering the exile history of the ANC and SWAPO*, Johannesburg: Jacana Media, 2009

Truth and Reconciliation Commission of South Africa Report, 5 vols, Pretoria: TRC, 1998

Twala, Mwezi and Ed Barnard, *Mbokodo: Inside MK: Mwezi Twala – A soldier's story*, Johannesburg: Jonathan Ball Publishers, 1994

Villa-Vicencio, Charles, *The spirit of freedom: South African leaders on religion and politics*, Berkeley: University of California Press, 1996

Internet sources

African National Congress: www.anc.org.za/

Pallo Jordan, Hani Memorial Lecture, 2003, www.sacp.org.za/main. php?ID=332

Padraig O'Malley interviews: www.nelsonmandela.org/omalley

Sheehan, Helena, interviews with Jeremy Cronin, 2001–2, webpages. dcu.ie/~**sheehan**h/za/**cronin**-aah01.htm and www.comms.dcu.ie/ **sheehan**h/za/**cronin**02.htm.

South African Communist Party: www.sacp.org.za

Truth and Reconciliation Commission: www.justice.gov.za/trc

Unpublished reports and dissertations

ANC, 'Report of the commission into recent developments in the People's Republic of Angola', 1984 (Stuart Report), available on *Heart of Hope* website

ANC, 'Report of a commission of inquiry set up in November 1989 by the National Working Committee of the National Executive Committee of the African National Congress to investigate the circumstances leading to the death of Mzwakhe Ngwenya (also known as Thami Zulu or TZ)', 1990 (Thami Zulu Report)

ANC, 'Report of the commission of enquiry into certain allegations of cruelty and human rights abuse against ANC prisoners and detainees by ANC members', 20 August 1993 (Motsuenyane Report)

Barrell, Howard, 'Conscripts to their age: African National Congress operational strategy, 1975–86', D.Phil. dissertation, Oxford University, 1993

Van Driel, Nicole, 'The Wankie Campaign', MA dissertation, University of the Western Cape, 2003

Film

Ken Kaplan (director), 'The life and times of Chris Hani', 1994

Internet sources

Niki.au Memorial Congress, www.uni-niki.au

Radio Bantu, Haiti Memorial Leftand, 2004, www.radiobantu.ain.au

Parting to a blog interview, www.razusoundtime.org.oy

spect and leftan, unle, bese with form, vigour, 2004, webs.ag

Allkava leed.m4u.4 group and chin.and www.c.u.mahu.de.en
sha.mahila/vreality.htm

Stan Auga, Communist Party www.servo.org.in

term.md.lec.millions/communition, www.truci.comz.er

Unpublished reports and disclosions.

ANC "Report of the Commission into certain developments in the
Reader Republic of Angeos, 1984." Stuart Report, Stuart ate on
the array (date s/date.

ANC "Report on . . . Commission of Inquiry set up in November 1985
by the National Working Committee of the National Executive
Committee of the African National Congress to investigate the
circumstances leading to the death of Thami Zulu (known as
known as Thami Zulu.6Ex 129), Thami Zulu Report.

ANC "Report of the Commission of enquiry into certain allegations
of cruelty and human rights abuse against ANC prisoners and
detainees . . . . " (compiler 20 August 1984 (Motsuenyane Report)

Randall Elwynof Dislocation to their age-ANC branch and conflicts
coperations systems, 1972-84," UBPC. September, Crept
an-serie 1989.

Allan Duin-Nicole: The "white Campaign, Mediterranean University
of the World, pres. 2002.

Film

Ken Kaunda directing: The liberaliquity of South Haiti. 1994.

Index

146

149